100 Ways to
Win NaNoWriMo

Other books in the *You're On!* Series

100 Ways to Shine in the Media Spotlight

Novels by Gail Hulnick

The Lion's Share of the Air Time
A Bird in the Sand
Sleeping Dogs Lie
Kangaroo Court
Resorting to Murder
Resorting to Larceny
Resorting to Fraud

100 Ways to Win NaNoWriMo

Gail Hulnick

WINDWORD GROUP

WindWord Group Publishing & Media
1083 N. Collier Blvd, #324
Marco Island, Florida 34145

ISBN 978-1-947527-21-8

Please contact the publisher regarding bulk orders, special events or speaking requests.
Email:
admin@windwordgroup.com

Dedicated to the late Ray Bradbury, who wrote *Fahrenheit 451* in
eighteen days

100 Ways to Win NaNoWriMo

GAIL HULNICK

"I write to discover what I know."
Flannery O'Connor

TABLE OF CONTENTS

INTRODUCTION

I read an article last year in which a writer scathingly denounced the idea of participating in National Novel Writing Month. Essentially, the opinion was that it's an artificial, gimmicky waste of time. This book came from my urge to argue. I also wanted to give you the benefit of my experiences, as you get ready to write a novel in thirty days.

Maybe, though, you haven't decided yet. If not, in a few minutes you'll read my take on the benefits.

But first, a little background. National Novel Writing Month, shortened to NaNoWriMo, has been attracting hundreds of thousands of writers every November since 1999. The challenge is to put down 50,000 words in thirty days. It's been a non-profit organization since the mid-2000s, and its website offers tools, structure, and community to assist the novelists on their path toward the goal.

In the Appendix, you'll find a report on the numbers of people who sign up and the numbers who finish the draft of their novel.

Not very many do that. It averages out to about eleven percent. Your reaction to that depends on your point of view, I suppose. You might think that eleven percent is actually quite a few.

I just know that I was surprised that it wasn't closer to three-quarters or even half of the registrants, and that's the second thing that sparked me to write this book. I wanted to argue with the writer (writers?) who disapprove of NaNoWriMo, and I wanted to offer something useful to those who would like to be in the eleven percent who do win.

I don't like to think of it in terms of success or failure. If you plunge in, to try to write a novel, that's a success, right there. The people who write for half of November or complete 20,000 words instead of 50,000+ haven't failed. They've had an experience, too.

But if the experience you want to have is the one where you greet December 1st with a NaNoWriMo victory in hand, this book is for you.

What does it take to win? It takes a finished draft of a novel of at least 50,000 words at the end of the month. It isn't a contest or an awards program, with judges or people's choices. You win if you don't stop.

I've done it twice. The first time was November of 2021, when I wrote a mystery novel titled *Sleeping Dogs Lie*. The whole experience worked so well for me that I signed up again, four months later, for Camp NaNoWriMo, which is held in April and again in July. The April novel is titled *Kangaroo Court*.

If you think I'm a prolific writer from way back, you're wrong. Writing a novel was one of my lifelong goals. If it's one of yours—maybe even a bucket list item—we are kindred spirits. I started and left unfinished quite a few novels, but eventually, I got serious about it and finished one. It was probably about forty years from the first one I started to the one I published. I had lots of writing practice over those years, and took many courses, but that doesn't add up to 'writing a novel'. You have to get to the point where you type The End.

Sleeping Dogs Lie was not the first novel I ever finished but I had never written one so quickly. Most of them took six months to a year and probably most will have that pace in the future.

But in that NaNoWriMo month I learned a lot about craft and about self-discipline that I've gone on to apply to the ones taking a year to write. It was far from a waste of time.

I like to compare it to different types of running. If you've done marathons or any long-distance running, you know about the preparation, the pacing, and the state of mind that go with that. But what's wrong with using your legs for a sprint once in a while?

NaNoWriMo is definitely a sprint. You'll have to have a good plan and some tools if you want to finish, and to win it.

This book has 100 tips to help you. It also contains the journals that I kept during each of the two NaNoWriMo projects I did, a list of resources for writers, and samples of outlines that I used to keep the momentum going.

Some of the tips may be controversial, and you might disagree with my suggestions. That's fine; take what works for you and leave the rest behind. If you're reading this for use with a class or a club doing NaNoWriMo together, the debatable tips could be a launchpad for group discussions.

If it's your first time signing up for NaNoWriMo, I hope you find the book useful and entertaining. If you've already done it and won it, I hope there's some déjà vu, plus a few new ideas here.

The 100 ways are not meant to be read in strict chronological order (although there's nothing wrong with doing that). But it also works if you dip into them one by one, randomly.

You may notice that the tips near the beginning are most helpful at the start of your preparation, whether a month out from November 1st or the day before. The ones in the forties, fifties, and sixties have a lot of focus on the need for motivation when you're slowing down in the middle, and the ones in the eighties and nineties tend to reflect the pace of the last week when you can see the finish line in the distance.

I'd love to hear any reactions you have, either in review form somewhere, in an email to me c/o the publisher, WindWord Group, or on social. And do check out the www.nanowrimo.org site. It hosts author profiles, promotes writer fluency and education, partners with libraries and community centers on events and forums, and encourages the love of the written word around the world.

Let's get started!

1

SET AN INTENTION

You're going to win it, right? Make up your mind. Don't put it on your calendar as a 'Maybe'. *"If I don't have a better option that day, and if the cat isn't sick, and if the weather is crummy, and if I'm feeling energetic, I* **might** *start this NaNoWriMo thing."*

No.

Make up your mind today that by November 30th, you will have 50,000 words done and the official NaNoWriMo Winner T-shirt on its way to your closet. And take the necessary steps to begin on November 1st. You can't bake a one-hour cake if you start the hour standing in your kitchen with no eggs and no sugar.

2

GIVE YOURSELF SOME ANTICIPATION TIME

Even before you gather the tools that you'll need to hit the ground running on November 1st, spend a little time getting your mind into gear. Picture yourself at your desk (or coffee shop counter or library table or wherever you plan to make the thing) and picture yourself concentrating on the pages or the screen for hours, days, and weeks. Because that's what it will take.

Anticipate the work you'll be doing, the thrills you'll have when it goes well and the depression, fear, or anger when it doesn't. I'm sorry if I'm making this sound like not much fun, but there *will* be bad days. The odds are higher that you'll push past them and keep going if they don't surprise you.

3

PLAN YOUR SCHEDULE

This novel-writing project is going to take some significant time this month. I'm not saying that you'll have to write sixteen hours a day, seven days a week—or maybe you will. I have no idea how fast a writer you are. Anthony Burgess wrote *A Clockwork Orange* in three weeks, the same length of time it took Jack Kerouac to write *On the Road*. (Just so you don't think I'm only a fan of fast writing, I'll mention that J.R.R. Tolkien spent sixteen years on *The Lord of the Rings*.) And yes, the word count in all of these varies.

I'm rambling—my point is that you know yourself and how fast you write, what type of book you want to write, whether you'll be doing this full time or on evenings and weekends around your day job. Make a plan for a daily word count goal.

4

ORGANIZE YOUR LIFE

Set aside the time you'll need to achieve that daily word count and get yourself across the 50,000-word finish line by November 30th. Ideally, you'll do at least 1,667 words a day, day in day out, and if you can be that steady, you'll get an extra badge. (More about the badges later.)

To have those hours alone to start and pump that stream of words, the people in your personal life will need to know something about what you're doing. What you'll need to do in your work life will vary, obviously, depending on what kind of work it is. But you will need to manage your time.

5

CHOOSE YOUR STORY IN ADVANCE

"I think I'd like to do a romantic drama about fighter pilots. No, wait, there's that idea I had about a mystery set in Venice. Oh, hang on a minute, my favorite novel last year was a paranormal about a young man searching for the true story of his real parents—"

No!

If you sit down November 1st in your first writing session and this is the way you're thinking, you'll still be there hours, even days later. Or you'll start the fighter jets novel, decide you don't like it, dream about canals and gondolas, then decide you'd rather do a high fantasy novel … and it will be November 15th before you really get started. Greet November 1st with all that preliminary thinking done and be ready to lay down those words from the very first hour.

6

CHOOSE YOUR WRITING SPACE

Where do you work best? If you don't know, NaNoWriMo prep could be the perfect time to find out. You could make a four-week plan—one week in your house, one week at a library, one week at a coffee shop, one week in a park. You could change it up every day, if you're really unsure (and have a lot of options).

Wherever and whenever you choose, once you've made the choice, settle into it. Think of the way a dog might ramble around, sniffing this and that, then once a spot is chosen, circles around following its tail two or three circuits, then collapses, often with a mighty sigh. It very rarely gets right up and goes to another spot, right away.

Choose your writing space and your tenure, then settle in.

7

SET UP YOUR TOTEMS

If Michael Jordan believed in wearing his UNC championship-winning shorts under his professional uniform for every game and Serena Williams brought her shower sandals to the court, who am I to bring skepticism to the subject of superstition or totems?

Finishing a major challenge like writing a novel is a mental test as much (and maybe, more) than anything else. You have to train your mind to get into the right state of confidence and determination, and having the right objects around you is important. Is it your favorite mug, the one that reads "Can I quote you on that?" Is it the quill pen you made yourself or a hat that you bought in San Francisco?

Even if you don't have a favorite mug or pen, spend a moment to choose a couple. You may not drink coffee and you might use your phone, instead of anything resembling paper, but having a mug and a pen close by is a nod to the tradition of novelists that you're joining. Mark Twain and his fountain pen. Hemingway with his Montegrappa and Salman Rushdie with his collection of vintage pens. Gertrude Stein, L. Frank Baum, Dorothy Parker, and Douglas Adams, with their numerous cups of coffee. You might want to put something stronger than coffee in your mug (and if you did, you'd join another long list) but I wouldn't advise it.

8

CHECK OUT THE NANOWRIMO WEBSITE

You'll find an incredible trove of advice and experience. The people there have been supporting and encouraging writers for many years and almost any question you might have about the rapid-writing challenge will be answered. You can also explore the many community and engagement possibilities, the webcasts and special events that have been scheduled for November, and the authors they have lined up to present to the crowd.

You can announce the project you'll be working on, too. Now, there's a moment when you'll be stepping up! Pick a specific date to make that announcement online and give it some ceremony. Celebrate afterward with your ritual of choice: a walk in the park or on the beach; a glass of wine or other beverage; a new pair of shoes; your favorite dinner. You are actually going to do this! November 1st, you'll be back on the NaNoWriMo website, recording your word count.

9

DECIDE ABOUT YOUR BADGES

As you track your progress through the month on the NaNoWriMo website, you'll automatically be given badges for various milestones you hit: recording your word count for two and three days in a row; reaching 5,000, then 10,000 words, finishing a week, two weeks, and so on. You might decide that you want to (or have to) get absolutely every badge that's available, and if so, you'll record your word count every day.

If you decide to go after every badge, you'll have to write a minimum of 1,667 words and record them every day. You won't be able to build in some flexibility for days you just have too many other obligations or come down with a flu bug. But you don't *have* to go after every badge. Do what works for you.

10

DECIDE HOW SOCIAL YOU WILL BE

The NaNoWriMo website gives you the opportunity to identify your geographic region and sign up to a group of other writers nearby. A volunteer coordinator stays in touch with you throughout the month. That's just one of the ways the experience can be made into a collegial, sociable time, with plenty of external motivation and encouragement. You can also create groups of friends that you connect with, daily or even hourly, if you wish. (For those of you who socialize online better if you are undercover, you can use a made-up name.)

It's entirely up to you and you know yourself best. But keep in mind your goal (and the focus of this book): winning NaNoWriMo. That means coming out of it with at least 50,000 words and the first draft of a novel. If you can do that AND chat with fifty-five friends throughout the day, go ahead. But if one of those has to go, it has to be the chatting.

11

DITCH THE BIRDS-EYE VIEW

When you think of the month as if from a distance, it might seem intimidating. When you break the goal sentence down, it might seem even more overwhelming. Write a novel in a month. *"Write a novel—are you kidding me? I've been wanting to do that since I was twenty, and I haven't done it yet. What makes me think I can handle it now?"*

And do it in a month? *"I can barely get enough groceries, keep myself in clean clothes, and clock my daily hours on the job in a month. How can I find the time to write down this idea that's been playing in my head for so long?"*

You need to do it one day at a time. Don't look at the NaNoWriMo landscape from high above and far away. Zoom in, as if you're a camera, and look at one specific day. Today, you will set the alarm early and get up; then, write for two hours or 2,000 words, whichever comes first. Or—today, you will get home from work, eat, clean up, have family time, or whatever; then, ignore the screen and that new movie on your best streaming service, and write for two hours (or however many it takes to get to 1,667).

12

GET YOUR PARTNER ON BOARD

As much as your spouse, lover, fiancé, fiancée, boyfriend, girlfriend, or partner supports you in your desire to be a novelist, unless they are writers themselves, they don't really know what it is you're doing or want to do. If they've never done NaNoWriMo themselves, they won't know what you're getting ready for or what the days will be like, once November is underway.

Tell them as much as you can and involve them in your experience. Let them help and support you, if they want to, and answer any questions they have.

13

GET YOUR FAMILY ON BOARD

Your partner might be your biggest fan, cheerleader, and confidante. But your parents, siblings, and children might be another fantastic source of support.

They also might be a roadblock, either literally, if they have plans for you that will steal the time you need to turn out those pages, or emotionally, if there are things they say, or opinions that you think they might have, that will drag you down, emotionally.

Talk to them, and let them know how much this means to you.

14

GET YOUR FRIENDS ON BOARD

Imagine yourself saying this to one of your friends: *"I'm going to write a novel in a month. In November, actually."* I have no idea how they are likely to respond, but I do know that the experience will work out better for you if you have at least one buddy you can talk with about how it's going, how you feel, and how important it is.

Don't let anybody jeer at you or coax you into putting your novel in the backseat while you ride up front with them. It's only a month. They can let you focus on this goal while a few other things slide. It's a time for putting yourself first and dedicating yourself to this task and this journey. Athletes do it all the time and so do entrepreneurs. Friends will support you.

15

DECIDE ABOUT YOUR WORD COUNT

You're more likely to succeed if you make a choice on this in advance. Yes, of course, you could wait and see how you do. If you've never measured your daily progress before, you might have no idea which is your natural output: 500 words a day or 5,000. I've met writers who think it's no big deal to write 10,000 or even 15,000 words a day. Those are numbers that leave me gulping for air. I can't even imagine.

16

BEWARE THE HOLIDAYS

Every month has some sort of holiday or special occasion coming up that might derail your commitment. U.S. Thanksgiving in November, yes; but then, there's Christmas and Hanukkah, New Year's Day, Valentine's Day, Easter, Passover, Ramadan, Fourth of July, Memorial Day, Kwanzaa, Diwali, Vesak, various Independence and National Days, shortest day of the year, longest day of the year (and my apologies to anyone I've left out). Then, there's your own birthday and those of your loved ones.

There is no particular month that could have been chosen that wouldn't have a pothole for somebody. Steer around them. Set aside some time, get up a little earlier, stay up a little later. You won't want to skip if you want to get that every-day-writing badge. And you won't want to skip a day in case you lose momentum.

17

PLAN YOUR WRITING PLACE(S)

Have some fun anticipating your physical location during NaNoWriMo, but keep in mind that you want to be somewhere that is conducive to starting and maintaining that word flow. The library, your home office, your backyard, a coffee shop—pick a place that has the seating arrangement, sound level, lighting, accessories, environment, humans nearby or solitude that you need.

It might not be just one place. Maybe you want to reward yourself at the end of each week, on November 15th, or on the last day with some sort of 'treat' location or special spot. Think about it now, make a plan, and you'll have one more motivation to keep writing if you have days when there is a lot of trouble coming up with even one sentence.

18

PLAN YOUR WRITING ROUTINE

Save your imagination and your spontaneity for your story. The more predictability you have in your daily writing routine, the less time you waste in thinking about whether you'll read yesterday's pages first, whether you'll take a break after one hour or two, and whether you like to finish the day's work in the middle of a scene.

19

PLAN YOUR MEALS

Oh, there are so many ways to distract yourself from writing! Food and drink are among the most compelling. *What's for dinner? Do I have all the ingredients or groceries that I need? Should I go to the store? Is that leftover pizza going to be enough? What did Charles Dickens eat while he wrote? I'm sure that information is available online somewhere. I'll just look it up …*

If you have the time, in October, you might even go so far as to make a thirty-day menu plan. Keep it simple and set aside a specific block of time for cooking. Stock up on the groceries you need and if you run out, enlist the help of one of those friends you brought on board in Tip 14. Plan to eat and drink something special on November 30th (or December 1st, if you just crash at the end of the month).

20

PLAN YOUR EXERCISE

You have to move, every day. You can't just sit there, in front of a desk, or lie down on a couch or bed, for thirty days. Walk, run, bike, swim, take a class—whatever refreshes you.

If you've never been in daily action before, start now, and that's one more positive thing you'll get out of NaNoWriMo.

21

CHOOSE YOUR TIME OF DAY TO WRITE

You might be constrained by your job or your family commitments. Fair enough. But it can be a useful exercise to take a weekend when you don't have too much going on and experiment with your rhythms and your preferences. If you can, do you like to get out of bed before dawn and go straight to your desk? Do you like to get out for some exercise, have some breakfast, and then sit down with your notepad or your computer? Are you a night owl, with a mind brimming with images and words in the evening?

There is going to be some time of your day when the writing comes easily. Half an hour in that time slot might give you more words than four hours in another.

22

DO THREE WORDS ON YOUR STORY IDEA

Woman becomes wife *(Pride and Prejudice)*. Day in Dublin *(Ulysses)*. Creature seeks magic *(Lord of the Rings)*. Wizards attend school—you get the point.

Another point this makes is just what a long road trip it is between an idea and a finished novel. For those who think that once you have a good idea you're done—that somebody else could just "write it up"—well, you're not, and they can't. And for those who think that if you see three words of your idea summing up someone else's fiction project, you've been robbed—you haven't.

23

DO THREE WORDS ON YOUR SETTING

In many of the best books, the setting functions like another character. Does your story take place in downtown wartime Paris? Ancient Roman countryside? New York today? 2122 on Mars? You will have many individual scenes set in different places but spend some of your prep weeks nailing down the overall setting—place and time.

24

DO THREE WORDS ON YOUR 'ABOUT'

Every novel is about something. War, peace, love, identity, family, redemption, success, failure, growth. One word is easy. Write three, and have them link to one another and use that to say what you need to say. War solves nothing. Peace is avoidance. Love always lasts. Success breeds success. Etc.

25

DO THREE WORDS ON YOUR CHARACTERS

Have fun with this. (and I'm not writing that sarcastically). Meet these people, introduce them to yourself and to imaginary others. You'll need three words on your protagonist and three on your antagonist. Insecure, brainy girl/bossy, bitter teacher. Overprotective, former cheerleader/nomadic, independent son. You can do various versions before you land on the phrase you'll bond with and take forward on November 1st. But keep it to three words on each, at this point. No thousand-word, stream-of-consciousness paragraphs. That comes later.

26

CHOOSE YOUR POINT OF VIEW AND TENSE

You're going to write this novel in the first, second or third-person point of view, singular or plural. "I went to L.A. to hide out." Or, "you went to L.A. to hide out." Maybe, he, she or they went.

You're going to choose a tense, present, past, or future. "I go to L.A. to hide out." "You go to L.A. to hide out" (ooh, that's sounding good.) "He goes to L.A. to hide out"—then what? Doesn't it just scream for a "but"? But his brother finds him in a day." Or whatever. Carrying on into the past and future, "he went to L.A.", "he will go to L.A." etc.

Play with the possibilities: each one will take your story in another direction. Sometimes, when a novel isn't working, you go back and re-do it in a different tense, or with a different point of view, and the stars will align. But you don't have time to do that, within thirty days. Make your choices during the preparation phase and stick to them. You can always try something different on the second draft.

27

CHOOSE YOUR BOOK'S TIME FRAME

Does the story take place in a day, a week, or a month? Over a lifetime? A day?

There are advantages and disadvantages to each. Make a choice now and if later in the month you begin to feel there's a better option, promise yourself to take it during the next draft.

28

DO A FIRST VERSION OF YOUR OUTLINE

Toward the end of this book, you'll find two of the outlines that I did for *Sleeping Dogs Lie*, version one and version twelve. I have an outline style that I've developed for myself over the years; if it works for you, too, you're welcome to use it. But you may have your own idea of the best outline. It might have fifty-four lines for fifty-four scenes, it might have three—beginning, middle, end. Maybe it's a diagram with circles, boxes, and arrows. Whatever works for you. Just get it out of your head and down on paper or on screen, before November 1st.

Use the outline writing as a step in finding out what your story wants to be.

29

DO A 25-WORD PLOT SUMMARY

Write a short narrative that tells your whole story, beginning, middle and end. Step back from it, for an hour or a few days or whatever, and then return to it. This will help you hone your idea and make you ready to write on November 1st. It also might be helpful, down the road, if you're writing a query letter to an agent or preparing to write a treatment for a producer.

Be specific, but leave enough imagination space for surprising yourself.

30

IMAGINE YOUR INCITING INCIDENT

Many authors find that working through their story as a movie is an effective way of preparing to write. Picture the opening image, picture your hero, picture the conflict.

Most movies are highly structured, with a time limit of seventy-five to a hundred and twenty minutes. Significant events or 'beats' occur in a pattern that move the story along.

They start with a set-up that shows the audience what 'normal' is, then blow everything up (metaphorically or literally) with an inciting incident that throws the main character into the story. Before November 1st comes up on the calendar, you should know what your inciting incident will be.

31

COUNT DOWN!
TEN DAYS TO GO!

Use something fancy and visual to make this into a game. Ten candles that you burn, one by one, perhaps. Ten pair of socks: wear one each day then toss in the hamper until you have none left and your thirty barefoot days of NaNoWriMo begin. Ten bobblehead dolls that you put on your dashboard then bring into the house, one by one, to sit around your desk. Choose something with meaning for you.

32

COMMIT TO WRITING CONTINUOUSLY

You will never win NaNoWriMo if you skip a lot of days and think you can catch up later. Even if you are the fastest, most prolific writer on earth, at some point you'll be unable to write enough words to make it to 50,000.

For example, if you miss a few days after starting November 1st, you might think you're still in the game. And you might be, if you only have five or six thousand words to make up, averaged over the next three weeks. But if you do this a few times, you could find yourself staring at a calendar that has you writing 10,000 words on each of the final five days.

Maybe you could do that, but why should you? Plan to do a reasonable number of words or hours each day, and commit.

33

BE DECISIVE

Even if you like to ramble through life, taking your time, avoiding black-or-white choices, and analyzing options endlessly, use NaNoWriMo as an experiment in being focused and determined. Decide on your story, your main character, your setting, and what it is you want to say, then go for it.

34

UNDERSTAND THAT THIS IS A FIRST DRAFT

It doesn't have to be perfect! In fact, it shouldn't be. Everyone's first draft sucks. I've heard some writers refer to it as the "puke draft". Just get it out there, and know that you will be revisiting it.

35

TAKE IT ONE DAY AT A TIME

Celebrate the completion of each. Mark it off on a checklist, cross it off on a calendar, or move the file with that day's writing into a folder. Yes, NaNoWriMo is about a word count and a finished novel, but the way to get there is to put in the time, day by day.

36

SET A TIMER FOR WRITING SPRINTS

This is a great hacknique for overcoming inertia. If you're blocked in some way or you've just fallen out of love with your story, do a writing sprint. Fifteen minutes, twenty minutes, whatever. Set a timer, force yourself to start typing when you press 'start', and go hard and fast until you hear that finishing bell.

37

TAKE BREAKS FOR CONGRATULATIONS

Pay attention to what you're achieving here. At the end of Day Seven, for example, if you're following the standard 1,667 words a day, heading for 50,000 words total, you've written almost 12,000 words. Well done!

Or—maybe you will look at it by story beats. By Day Seven, you've thrown your main character into great personal danger, coaxed her out of the cave she retreated to, and put her on the bus to a new country. All this hard work is paying off! Mad props to you.

38

WRITE FULL SENTENCES AND PARAGRAPHS

This is a mistake I made, and I learned from the experience. When I didn't have any full inspiration for a next scene or a transition or some dialogue, I put down, in point form, whatever thoughts I had, usually along the lines of "Lillian argues with Ted" or "Lillian argues with herself".

That's not writing a novel, that's doing an outline. It left me with a lot of blanks to fill in later.

No bullet points!

39

DO ABSOLUTELY NO PROOFREADING

It's okay if you want to reread a few pages from the previous day, to get yourself up to speed and into the right lane, but resist the urge to proofread or stew over punctuation. That is left-brained thinking: analytical and methodical. For this first draft, you want right-brained thinking going on: creative and artistic.

If you happen to see that you've misspelled 'bloodthursty', leave it there. You or your editor will catch it another day. It will also make you more intense about your proofreading on later drafts, knowing that there probably is quite a bit to catch!

40

DO VERY LITTLE EDITING

Editing and proofreading are the quicksand in the front yard of your first draft. If you allow yourself to wade into it, you'll be there forever. With my first novel (not a NaNoWriMo project), I wrote and rewrote my first page about three hundred times. It took me years to finish that book.

Keep a side file where you note any ideas you have for editing, major or minor. It might be a significant revision; for example, maybe you think you should get rid of the first forty pages because your story really begins when the main character leaves home and you don't need all those pages about his struggle to make that decision. It might be copyediting; for example, you notice that you begin every paragraph with the word "I" and you want to change that up.

At the end of the month, you'll have a substantial list of editing ideas, and that will give you a terrific starting point for your next draft.

41

PRINT OUT PAGES AT THE END OF EVERY DAY

If I had to mention only one move to seal the deal on getting this novel done, it would be this. On past projects, I've tried various ways of ending a day's writing. Saving a file, obviously. Doing a computer backup. Moving files into a folder.

Sometimes, when I reached the end of a first draft, I would print out all three hundred pages plus. It always seemed to take an unreasonably long time (although I did like the look of that big stack of paper).

Printing pages day by day is a good compromise. You get the satisfaction of seeing that stack grow, but you don't have to wait until the end to see pages. And despite the convenience, efficiency, and lower cost of keeping everything on a computer desktop, somehow it seems more like a book when it's printed on something you can touch.

42

ENJOY THE BADGES ON THE WEBSITE

Writing is hard work. The badges turn it into a bit of a game.

It's not a game, of course. You're putting hours of your life into it, not to mention your emotions, your heart, and your soul. As Ernest Hemingway once said, "All you do is sit down at a typewriter and bleed."

Take it seriously but try to find the fun in it, too. That helps many writers to keep the balance.

43

UPDATE YOUR WORD COUNT EVERY DAY

Until I actually got into the midst of it, it sounded silly to me, collecting badges for counting words and working every day. But it did help with the motivation. I don't know—maybe there's an element of addictive behavior to it, but you can't really assess it till you've tried it.

There is a badge that you only get if you update your word count every day. This is the one that will help you maintain the discipline.

44

UPDATE WORD COUNT THROUGHOUT THE DAY

If you wait to the end of the day, something might come up to distract you or prevent you from recording your word count that day—and then that's a badge you don't collect.

You can do the update on the NaNoWriMo website as frequently as you want during a day.

45

MAKE IT TO YOUR DAILY WORD COUNT

Again, another badge you won't get, if you don't follow this tip. Of course, you might find other reasons to let your daily production ebb and flow. If you pour out 5,000 words one day and just manage a dribble of 200 the next, that's up to you. But if you're looking for ways to solidify a daily discipline, the badge quest helps.

46

AFTER WEEK ONE, MAKE A REWARD CHART

Many writers notice that their motivation flags after the first week. If that's you, make a list of twenty-three daily rewards you can offer yourself. An hour off at a park or a beach. A festive season coffee. Your favorite dessert. A new shirt. A bottle of good wine. A visit to a bookstore to buy the book you'll read in December. An hour of listening to your favorite music.

Hang it where you can see it.

47

RECOMMIT TO YOUR EXERCISE PLAN

If you are twenty-five, you probably can get away with sitting at work all day then immediately opening your novel-writing file and getting into three or four or more hours of writing. And more sitting. But if you do that for thirty years, you'll have problems. Your body won't like it.

Sitting is the new smoking. You have to move your body, moderately or intensely, for at least an hour a day. Find something you like to do—run, swim, play tennis, do yoga, walk, ride a bike—and fit it in, every day.

48

REPORT TO SOMEBODY

This could be a writer friend who is doing NaNoWriMo at the same time or someone you know only online, through the website forums. If your relationship with your spouse, your parents, or your siblings works well in this direction, it could be someone close to you. Whoever it is, set it up as some sort of reciprocal arrangement. This person will be your accountability partner.

Pay attention to your reaction to this, and view it as an experiment only, over the first few days. If you find yourself becoming rebellious or feeling resentful about reporting to someone else, then stop doing it. Find another way to keep yourself on track.

49

ARE YOU VISUAL?
DRAW A MAP

This could be fun. Might be a detailed atlas type of map, with place names given to each of the thirty days. Might be a fantasy-world type of map, with a red line to show the route, as you take it, through the month. Might be a thirty-mile map of some place you know well that's close to home.

Make it colorful, make it quirky, make it yours.

50

ARE YOU AUDITORY?
PICK A SONG

This is your 'champions' song. Play it every day at the beginning and the end of your writing session. Sing along, loud and proud. Dance. Loosen up. It will help your writing.

51

CREATURE OF HABIT? PICK A ROUTINE

Start and finish in the same chair every day. Eat the same food and sip the same drink. Let your superstitious side roam free.

52

NEED VARIETY? LIST YOUR OPTIONS

Work in a different location (coffee shop, park, library) every day. You may be one of the writers who is more successful if no two days are alike.

Know yourself.

53

DO THE NEXT OUTLINE

At the back of this book, I've included the first outline I did for *Sleeping Dogs Lie* and the twelfth. You'll see that there are a lot of changes. If we drill down on the vocabulary, we may find that we're using similar methods, just calling them by different names. My 'pantsing' or 'discovery writing' happens within the rows and columns of an outline table. I find that if I don't note the ideas down in the outline that I lose the thread of them from one scene to the next.

You might find that you don't need an outline and that having one steals some of the joy and surprise of the writing. That's cool. You do you. But if you do use outlines, make sure you save carefully and always work from the most recent.

54

DITCH THE OUTLINE

Maybe you were meant to be a discovery writer. The outlines worked for me and I found that as the days went by, I was pouring out a stream of sentences. But if you're a week or so into the month and you're either spending too much time polishing and changing an outline or you're just not getting anything at all, consider pivoting to the 'do it by the seat of your pants' approach of the pantser.

A compromise between the two would give you the name 'plantser'.

55

SET A TIMER ON YOUR STARING INTO SPACE

Mentioned earlier, but worth a number of its own. Daydreaming, staring into space, and letting your mind play are important parts of the creative process.

But if you feel you are wasting too much time, limit your wool-gathering (Odd word. Apparently, it comes from the 16th century and refers to a trade in tufts of wool that sheep leave behind on fences. No explanation as to why it has anything to do with daydreaming.)

Set a timer, give yourself ten to fifteen minutes for mental meandering, then get those fingers tapping on the keyboard and those pages piling up.

56

PLAN THE SCENE YOU WILL WRITE TOMORROW

This is particularly useful if you tend to show up at the desk at the beginning of your writing session and stare at the screen with no idea where to go next. Do the planning just after you've finished writing for the day and have it happen mostly in your imagination. Keep any note-making to a minimum.

57

DREAM

If you can, put your next-day, first-scene-to-write into your mind as the last thing you think about before going off to sleep. You might find that your subconscious helps you overnight.

58

CALIBRATE GENRE AND SUBGENRE

Spend as much time as you need to, during the preparation month, in getting clear and staying clear on your genre. Every novel fits into some genre somewhere. Even if it's about nothing and nothing happens: it might be literary fiction (and it might be not a novel at all, and ripe for some rethinking). If you think it's a little bit of a lot of things (*it's mysterious but there's a love affair in the middle but then the spy agency reveals the list of all the undercover agents—*), choose one of the genres to situate it. Maybe it's a mystery, maybe it's romantic drama, maybe it's an espionage or a political thriller. Maybe urban fantasy, maybe historical romance. Pick one.

Clarifying this in your thinking will make it easier to get that flow of words and pages happening. After it's all done, and you reread it, you might want to reclassify and change it. But the important thing is to have something, to create something that you can change. If it's only in your mind or your imagination, and not yet on paper or screen, then you haven't written it.

59

PLAY WITH TITLES

Some writers are superstitious, and save the naming of their novel to the very last minute. Some have to have a title before they even begin to create their protagonist.

If you fall somewhere in the middle, writing and rewriting a title can be a good way to break through any indecision about a plot or character development. It can be a productive distraction and a way to pass a little time while waiting for the next surge of paragraphs to begin.

60

DO MANY PAGES ON YOUR CHARACTERS

Do you remember back to Tip 25 when you were doing three words only on your protagonist and antagonist? Now is the time to dig deep on your prep ideas for your major characters, your setting, and your themes. Write as many details as you can and add to your list of traits and features whenever you've finished writing for the day. Imagine the characters in various situations. Put them into imaginary scenes. Hear their voices, see their clothes, watch them move.

61

IMAGINE YOUR NOVEL AS A LINE GRAPH

Identify the important points or beats of the story. Space them out on the x-axis. The y-axis could be rising action or emotional tone or any aspect you want to highlight. Think about this and play with the points and lines only until you feel a flood of words coming on. Then, put it aside and get back to writing.

62

DRAW A PICTURE OF THE CHARACTER ARCS

If you are an artist or if you simply like to doodle, keep a sketch book and capture your ideas about the way your protagonist and antagonist look. Draw whenever the writing needs a little help.

Just to be clear, this tip is intended to help if you're having trouble with scene ideas, dialogue, transitions, or pacing. If the words are flowing, don't stop to do any of this picture-drawing, line-graphing, or background thinking. Just write.

63

MANAGE YOUR MINOR CHARACTERS

Minor characters can be the herd of cats that race around your manuscript, defying your efforts to make them part of a good story. The worst case is when one of them is so compelling that they start to take over and become the main character.

Make sure they know their place. If you find yourself writing a long scene where a minor character's backstory or arc is the focus, finish it, then save it to a new document. It might be another novel, someday.

64

SET UP A 'PARKING LOT'

Put your new ideas and distractions there. Have you ever been cruising along, making progress on your story, and suddenly been struck by a new idea? It can feel like the best idea you've ever had and you may be tempted to throw out everything you've been working on to make way for this newcomer.

Bad idea. New ideas often seem shinier than the ones we've lived with for a while. But dropping the current project means that you'll never know how it turns out and you'll never get to The End. Do that enough times and you'll never finish a book.

Don't blow off this new idea, but put it into another file that you'll open later, after NaNoWriMo is done.

65

DON'T GET STUCK

Even if you have doubts about whether you'll keep any of these words or pages, keep on writing. This is your first draft and you might end up changing a lot of it, but for now, these are your pages and these are your words.

None of it is 'bad'. It's all practice.

66

RESIST THE URGE TO COMPARE

Your first draft is not the same as somebody else's number one bestseller. Most of those novels that you buy and read have been revised repeatedly, then copyedited and proofread by a team of avid readers.

Imagine you play the piano or like to paint. Would you expect the music you play or the paintings you make to compare to Billy Joel on stage at Madison Square Garden or Vincent van Gogh at the Louvre? Don't beat up on yourself if you are feeling that your novel isn't coming out onto the page as well as you imagined it or as perfectly as some other book you admire.

67

DON'T THROW ANYTHING AWAY

Even if you can't use them in this novel, they might belong somewhere else. You have a career, not just one book.

68

MAKE STICKY NOTES

Put them up around your writing room or on your computer or phone. They can be inspirational quotes, ideas for your characters, or notes about your own reactions to things going on during NaNoWriMo. It doesn't matter what they are, specifically. It's the visual motivation that's important. Making a handwritten note is visual and tactile, and can help you stay focused.

69

EVERY CHARACTER NEEDS A GOAL

If you're finding the middle days of November are dragging and your daily word count is declining, give yourself a boost by revisiting your character chart. Look at each one of them, even the minor ones that barely qualified to receive a name, and ask yourself *"What do they want?"*

70

EVERY SCENE NEEDS CONFLICT

That's what makes a story. Stuff happens, people engage. If every character has a goal, it's only a matter of time before their goals collide and sparks fly.

71

FALL IN LOVE WITH YOUR STORY AGAIN

At various points during the month, many writers run out of gas. For some, it's the last few days. For others, it happens around Week Three. Maybe for you, on the second day!

Zoom in on your story again. Write a two-page summary of it. Tell it out loud. Open the recording app on your phone or computer, tell the story, then play it back, and really listen to it. Ask yourself this question: What's cool about my story?

Believe in it.

72

USE THE POWER OF YTC

The initials stand for "yet to come". Use this acronym when you're flying along through the words and pages. You don't want to slow yourself down or let yourself stop because you can't decide whether Main Character eats a steak or a salad (unless that's essential to the outcome of the scene). You don't want to slow down to name the street where the lovers are meeting, decide what exotic laws the fantasy world you're building enacted five years ago, or research how many hours it takes to drive from L.A. to San Francisco.

A few pauses for these sorts of things won't hurt, but beware letting details suck up all your writing time. When you get to the need for a detail and the word or phrase doesn't come to you immediately, just write YTC and fill it in later. I'm not saying 'don't put in details'. These are often the elements that make a story sing. Specific is better than general. Readers remember necessary details. Just don't get hung up on finding the perfect phrase right now. Use YTC.

73

WATCH FOR CAUSE AND EFFECT

Every action has a reaction, and every reaction can be traced back to an action. In some novels, the relationship may be obscure, but it's still there. There might be long gaps between, but you should be able to track the actions and reactions.

Use a chart, a line graph, a table, or a map, if that helps.

74

GET UNSTUCK ON MAKING UP NAMES

Some writers use up huge chunks of their writing time, dithering over names. It's true that a character name is very important. It has to fit and feel right. But most of us have a limited store of first and last names in our memory bank and we risk using the same ones repeatedly, if we write more than one novel. Also, you might reject many of the names you think of because they're the same as your second cousin's or one of your co-worker's.

Make use of the time you spend watching movies on TV. As the credits roll, make notes in a column of the first names that jump out at you. Then, in a separate column, list last names that you notice. Mix them up so that you're never just picking up a real person's name, first and last.

75

CHECK THE NAMES YOU'RE USING

Before you've used it too often, or become devoted to a particular name for your main character, research it online. This is one situation when stepping away from the writing to do research is a good idea. Google the name, check it on the movie database, and search it on a few sites or social platforms.

While broadly speaking you can't copyright a name or a title, some names are protected by trademarks and can't be used. Even if that isn't the case, many names are so well-known and carry so much baggage, that you risk letting your reader ascribe all sorts of traits and motivations to your main character that you don't want. Plus, if you ever meet the original user of that name socially, it won't go well.

76

ORDER THE
WINNER T-SHIRT

If you're past the 30,000-word mark, you're close enough. You don't want to be disappointed. Just in case there's a supply chain issue, or shipping is slow, you can go ahead and order the T-shirt. It will be on its way and you will have that knowledge in the back of your mind, during these last weeks.

Then, when it arrives, you can look at it in your closet, use it as a daily motivation, and get ready to wear it November 30th.

If you don't get to 50,000 words, don't wear it. Save it for next November.

77

TAKE BREAKS

As you get closer to the finish line, you're also getting closer to the climax of your story. You may find that you're excited to be telling it. You think about it constantly and while you are sitting at your laptop, you lose track of the time. The keyboard draws your hands, wrists, and fingertips like a magnet. You pound away for hours and hours and hours.

No.

Sitting nonstop is not good for your body or your mind.

78

RESIST PERFECTIONISM

Perfect is the enemy of good. The quest for it also leads to negativity and self-doubt. If you let it, perfectionism can paralyze you.

Your first draft won't be perfect and you should be okay with that. Work on believing that you are writing this novel for yourself. Don't focus on the judges or the haters, or imagine the criticism they might send your way. You aren't writing to please them or anybody other than yourself.

If **you** think it's good, or that it's 'perfect', then it will be.

79

TURN OFF THE DISTRACTIONS

If you are someone who hates to be disconnected, fine. Keep your phone at your side and your computer logged in to whatever sites and platforms are your constant companions through the day.

But you will find that your writing sessions run better and the words come more easily if you turn off email notifications, log off your internet browser, and put your phone in another room.

Schedule breaks to check your messages, if you must, but put at least an hour in between each break. We are all used to being constantly and instantly "on call" but there is no real reason to be.

80

RESIST THE URGE TO WRITE THE WORDS THE END

When you're into the fourth week, you may be tempted to write those magic words. Just to motivate yourself. Just to see how they look on the page. Because that is where you want to be. So much you can **taste** it.

You'll just be kidding yourself, and you know it. You have a lot more work to do. If you are slogging through the muddy middle and you need something to bring back your joy, write a two-page resolution scene.

81

USE POSITIVE SELF-TALK

You can do this. It is a good story. It is a GREAT story. So what if you've tried twelve times and you've never finished a novel? You're going to finish this one!

82

DEAL WITH SELF-DOUBT

If this is your twentieth novel, you might feel quite confident that you can finish. But if it's your first, you might have to do battle every day with the inner critic telling you it won't happen and that you aren't a writer.

Banish that imposter syndrome. You *are* a writer. Find other voices louder than the doubter—an encouraging teacher, a writer-buddy, a supportive writer group, a spouse or partner who's on your side. Lean on them and listen to them.

83

WATCH THAT PILE OF PAGES GROW

Of course, you will count them, but it can be fun to measure the pile. Even fifty pages make an impressive sight, sitting on the desk, and the two hundred pages that hold 50,000 words, double-spaced, are a handful, easily.

But how many inches or centimeters is that? I don't know. You'll have to write them, print your pages, and measure that stack yourself.

84

RESIST THE URGE TO TELL THE STORY TO ANYONE

Most of us are asked, at some stage and by someone, what we're working on. Work on a short description, like the 'elevator speech' people use for business. *"It's a mystery about a newspaper columnist in Florida who chases down the creep who is hurting dogs in her town."*

Don't go much farther than that. For one thing, people don't really want to know. Even more important, in telling the story to someone, you might use up the energy better spent on actually writing. You also might get reactions and comments you'd rather not hear.

Make an exception if it's a teacher or a writing group where you've agreed to share pages at milestones along the way.

But don't open yourself to comments so early in the process. Get that story finished and on paper. Stay focused on protecting the momentum.

85

POLISH THE PLOT POINTS

A novel is more than just 50,000 words, strung together. You need compelling characters and you need to have something to say. You also need STORY, and working with plot points will help you tell it (and show it) in the best way you can. In your non-writing hours, re-read a few blogs or books about narrative: beginning, middle, end; inciting incident; Act One turning point; midpoint; Act Two 'all-is-lost moment; climax; and resolution.

86

RESIST THE URGE TO START OVER

For many writers this is an urge comparable to the urge to edit someone else's draft. If that isn't an impulse you ever have, maybe think of your reaction to a late-night slice of pizza after you've already had a full meal, too many beers at the end of ten hours of manual labor, or an expensive dress in a store window that you are convinced will change your life.

It might seem like something you want to do in the moment, but it's a bad idea.

87

DON'T DO ANY OTHER WRITING

Of course, you might have to (or want to) write something else, at some other point in the month. Maybe emails to your mother, notes to your spouse, reports for work, long posts on social media.

Do any other writing after you have your word count for the day, if you can. If you do your NaNoWriMo writing in the evening or overnight, take a break before you begin. Go for a walk, take a nap, have a long conversation. The goal is to begin your fiction-writing session feeling fresh and eager to write something.

88

DON'T DROP OUT

Even if you're sick, you could just do a token fifty or one hundred words in that day. You won't get all the badges but you won't give up!

And you will finish and win.

89

CHOOSE YOUR 'AFTER-DAY'S-WRITING' TREAT

Although most authors read voraciously, some are very careful about what they read while in the middle of a fiction project of their own. It's not a concern about plagiarism, so much as a need to make sure that the style, tone, and voice of another writer doesn't seep into your work, almost without you noticing. You want to be original, not derivative.

One way to control for this is to relax with other art forms in the evening hours (or morning, if you are a late night, or all-night writer). Watch a movie or contemplate the work in a gallery or on your walls. Think about the effort other writers and creators have put into those things and feel yourself one of the compadres.

90

PREPARE FOR THE BLAHS

Many writers have ups and down during NaNoWriMo. Expecting a dip into the blues can be half the battle in defeating them.

Have rewards ready for making your word goal that day. Extra-special rewards might be an even better idea.
.

91

REMIND YOURSELF THAT IT'S A FIRST DRAFT

As you get into the last few days of the month, you might look back over your chapters and feel that they don't measure up to your dreams or expectations when you began the novel.

Maybe you have a favorite novel and you're deciding that despite all your hours of work, yours just isn't the same.

If you want to, you'll have plenty of future hours to revise and improve it. The important thing is not to get discouraged and to finish this one.

92

USE NANOWRIMO WRITING PROMPTS

Writing prompts can be a terrific tool to get yourself rolling when the words won't come. You can find them in many places, but using the ones on the NaNoWriMo site bring you even more into sync with the whole experience.

93

TAKE A DAY AT A TIME

As you get closer to the finish line, it can become harder to keep pushing. You may be exhausted, or filled with self-doubt about the quality of your story and the value of the time you've spent.

Tighten the focus on your calendar. Don't give up! Take it step by step. If you can just get those 1,667 words today, you can think about the ground you still have to cover some other time.

94

BE SELF-AWARE

Understand the psychology and the low moments that might make you lose motivation. Prepare for them.

Sometimes it's just the 'blahs'. But sometimes it's more than that. It's fear, self-doubt, or imposter syndrome. Sometimes it's an urge to escape. Recognize the feeling, identify it, and then let it go.

At the same time, don't let yourself lean over into too much self-confidence. Keep the balance.

95

SPEND TIME IN NATURE

This is one of my favorite solutions to any problem and the best way to prevent stress. We often are so busy and have so many goals and activities that we don't notice that it's been weeks since we were anywhere but in our home, in a vehicle, or in a workplace.

Find a park, a beach, or a hillside. Walk. Or simply, be there.

96

TELL YOURSELF THE STORY

Out loud. You'll probably fall in love with your story again, and you should hold onto that feeing.

But, at this stage, also listen for any huge problems. Characters you describe enthusiastically at the beginning who disappear before the end. Settings that made sense in the first chapter and don't, by the last. Motivations that aren't clear.

All of these are things that can be fixed in the last chapters.

97

TAKE NOTE OF THE HIGHS

When, where, and why do you actually **enjoy** writing? Pull this to 'top of mind'. It sometimes sinks to the bottom when we are balancing projects, publishing, goals, deadlines, business, and personal priorities. The pressure of pushing through to the final day of NaNoWriMo can overwhelm the reason you started on this journey in the first place.

If you don't enjoy it, don't do it. It's not a quick and easy road to being rich or famous. Writing and publishing a novel won't help you become a social media influencer or add to your follower count. It won't add to your brand. It's not a therapeutic tool to prove something to your high-school English teacher.

If you're doing it because you enjoy writing, most of the time, focus on those times and make sure you foster that feeling of joy.

98

RECOGNIZE THE LAST DAY OF WRITING

Wear the t-shirt you bought to memorialize this remarkable experience as a NaNoWriMo winner. Buy yourself a special coffee, tea, or breakfast to start the day. Give yourself permission to hang out on social media for a little longer than usual. If you're comfortable with this, and haven't told the world about it yet, tell people that you've just finished writing a novel.

Type The End.

99

DOCUMENT YOUR VICTORY

Take a photograph of the pile of pages, or the words The End on the computer screen, or you in your Winner t-shirt.

Send it out on whatever social media you use. Share with your writers' group, your NaNoWriMo pals, or friends you'd like to surprise with news of what you've been up to.

100

CELEBRATE!

It's the end of November 30th! Celebrate with a favorite drink, calls or texts to friends, a gift for yourself, a dance, a walk in the woods, a run on the beach, a weekend of sleep.

Winners feel like winners. You are a winner if you feel like one.

Congratulations!

MY NANOWRIMO JOURNAL November 2021

D o you keep a daily journal? I usually don't. I'd rather use my writing energy for projects like novels, short stories, and travel books.

But a friend suggested that keeping a journal during NaNoWriMo could be a good motivator for reinforcing the daily writing practice, and that it could be a nice souvenir of the experience, too.

These are the notes I made during November 2021 and April 2022.

Monday, November 1, 7:36 a.m.

I am going to win NaNoWriMo!

Can I write a novel in a month? Tens of thousands of others have. Why shouldn't I?

This National Novel Writing Month, founded by Chris Baty, began July 1, 1999 with twenty-one people in the San Francisco Bay area. The idea was for a group of writer/friends to help each other finish their novels. It has grown into an international event, with hundreds of thousands of people registering each time. It's also a non-profit organization with a mission to support writers and writing activities, year-round.

My husband, David Stone, calls it *Novelember*. I like that.

I signed up for NaNoWriMo on October 19th of 2021. I've been circling two or three ideas for new novels all year. I've written and finished novels before, but for some reason (perhaps a focus on my mother's illness) I haven't been able to start anything new in a few years. I finished a collection of short stories that all came from earlier days.

For this NaNoWriMo month, I decided to write a novel about one of my "media ladies", Lillian Howe. About six years ago, I published the first in a series of Media Mysteries, each one about a different woman in a different stage of life, working in a different medium: *The Lion's Share of the Air Time* was about 24-year-old Chelan Montgomery, a television news reporter; *A Bird in the Sand* featured forty-something Nevada Leacock, doing script-doctoring on a movie production. Now, I was planning *Sleeping Dogs Lie,* about 77-year-old Lillian Howe, chasing a killer using her newspaper column.

It's within the spirit of NaNoWriMo to come in with a well-constructed outline, a character list and sketches, and ideas about themes. The point of the month-long exercise is to get beyond that stage and into actual laying down of the words.

Fifty thousand of them, to be exact. Some writers go into NaNoWriMo planning to do 60,000 or 80,000 or 100,000—whatever their definition of a full, finished novel is.

I figure 50,000 is a good first goal for me.

I have been feeling really eager about this new addition to the series, although quite intimidated and blocked at the same time. When I saw the notification about NaNoWriMo, a light bulb went on. I'd heard about doing Novel Writing Month in the past, from time to time; I have a novel I want to stop delaying on; and I'm in a mood to do something *fast,*

Maybe that's because of following Formula One racing this year. Watching all those drivers go 250 mph—yes! I can do a novel in a month.

To "win" NaNoWriMo, I need 50,000 words by the end of November. I've set my private goal higher: I want 70- to 80,000 words in this novel. It will depend, partly, on what the novel shows me it wants to be, as we get rolling along together. I have an outline with three parts thought out; I know what happens at the beginning and the end; and the middle is just murky.

I'm feeling quite excited to be starting this. David is really interested in it, too, and wants to know what he can do to support and encourage me.

Right now, he's out, getting me a pumpkin spice latté to start the first day.

I have no doubt about succeeding at this. At NaNoWriMo, they call it a win if you reach the goal and finish the novel. You aren't competing with anyone else and no one is judging which novel is 'better' than any other.

I assumed that most people reach the goal, but apparently, I was wrong. I looked it up, and only about 11 percent finish. So, I guess 'win' isn't too outrageous a word.

They have a store, selling branded mugs, stickers, posters, etc. And T-shirts. One of them reads NaNoWriMo Winner, and there was an email in October, inviting you to preorder. Hah!

I guess that's one way to motivate yourself on November 1st and think positive from the beginning.

Another is to fall in love with your story.

Day 2

So, am I a plotter or a pantser? Writers like to discuss this. Do I make an elaborate outline, detailing character biographies and colorful descriptions of every setting before a single word is actually written?

Or do I fly 'seat of the pants'? I think this is an old-time aviator's expression. I'll have to look it up sometime.

But not now. I'm trying to change my habit of grabbing my phone each time I am curious about something that a search engine could answer. No question, it's a wonderfully useful invention, and it's very satisfying to be able to get a fact instantly. But the tradeoff is that you become increasingly reliant on the phone—almost tied to it. I interrupt what I'm doing, a conversation I'm in, dates I'm on, to reach for the phone because I want to know whether Zurich is east or west of Geneva. I don't *need* to know. I just have this habit.

But it is turning me into an easily distractible human being, and more so, every day. It also sometimes ruins the conversational flow with the other person, or even hurts their feelings.

And—wow. Look how far I'm been drawn away from the topic where I started: Plotter vs. Pantser.

So, I want to learn to be comfortable with not knowing the answers to questions instantly. Take that, Mr. Google!

I have always used outlines for every kind of writing: nonfiction, fiction, essays, term papers, columns, scripts, blogs, courses. Sometimes, they are quite broad: A. Introduction; B. Middle; C. Conclusion.

Sometimes they're really detailed. For this NaNoWriMo project, because I know I want to get at least 1,667 words a day, I decided to do a complex outline. It's in table form, with columns for Scene Number, Chapter, What Happens, Part of Act Number, Beat, Date Finished, Word Count, Page Count.

There will be 50 to 54 scenes, depending on how long or flashy the climax turns out to be. Also, the resolution might be short or long. I won't know those things until I get to those scenes … and that's the 'pantser' part.

On many writing blogs, they talk about 'plantsers'. This is somebody who plots, somewhat, then goes seat-of-the-pants, within the boundaries of the outline. I think that's me; I'm a plantser.

My outline for *Sleeping Dogs Lie* has already changed dramatically, after just one day of writing. The opening scene is the same, but in the second scene, when I want to show my main character's false belief about her world, the character I've chosen to be her mirror, her 'sounding board', and the vehicle for the main character realizing the truth, isn't yet in the story.

It wouldn't work to have her inserted here, so I have to find another way to do this.

A few adjustments to the outline ... and she can make her appearance in another way.

It's a weird process, to analyze the (slowly) unfolding action and put in all of the characters and elements that need to be there, all the while trying to avoid being clunky or awkward about it. Maybe the very experienced novelist does this intuitively, and therefore is able to be a pantser?

Maybe most of us, if we just sit down and write whatever comes out, pantser-style, end up with an unwieldy mess that has to be shaped into something people can read?

Day 3

So, now I'm beginning to have an understanding of why only eleven percent finish.
Ha.

If I hadn't made up my mind so decisively (and if I hadn't told so many people), I would be so tempted today to throw in the towel and quit.

Or, at least, take the day off.

The trouble with that is that one day off can turn into two or three. Then, I'd have to make up ground in the following days, to have any hope of finishing the novel in the month. I'd be looking at trying to do 5,000, 8,000, or even 10,000 words in a day!

Ha.

The solution is not to backslide. Keep up with the daily goal and the daily tally.

I already have a total of thirty-two pages sitting on my desk. I am printing a hard copy of each day's writing, using double spacing and sixteen-point font, for ease of editing later on. I think, at that rate, I'll have about 450 pages of this first draft by November 30.

The detailed outline has been a big help. Even though the weak parts of my brain (and emotions) are whining about quitting or taking a day off, the other parts are excited about getting on with this. Today, I am going to write Scenes 5 and 6, when Lillian makes her first visit (in the time frame of the story) to a local beach that welcomes off-leash dogs. Something happens that goads her into writing a newspaper column about the dog killing.

I don't know yet what that something will be.

The detailed outline grows more shades and tones every hour. I've been adding more rows and columns to the table (and taking some out.) I think I'll do an Appendix that shows the original outline and the one I ended up with, after all the revisions.

Outside my window, I can see the swimming pool, already filling up with swimmers, even though it's only eight a.m. There's one man there in blue bathing trunks and a lime-green shower cap.

I think he might make his way into my story, somehow.

But … on second thought … that's not the tone I'm going for, in this novel. I find I'm having to work to keep it serious and mysterious. I've been writing other novels for the *Resorting* series in the past few years and those novels have a much lighter tone. I've been trying to find some humorous touches for almost every chapter, put in some word play, and some wonky characters.

Now that I've turned back to the *Media Mysteries* series (this one, *Sleeping Dogs Lie,* is Book 3) I have to remind myself and get myself into the headspace of being more serious.

I think, after this, I will pick a lane and stay in it.

One of the reasons I wanted to do NaNoWriMo was to get myself into writing and finishing novels faster. In the past, I've tended to pick up, then put down a project, and sometimes I've lost the thread so completely that I never finish. Sometimes, I've changed, as a person, and my interests, observations, even opinions have changed. The story isn't what it would have been if I'd finished it two or three years earlier.

I have a couple like that from the 2013 to 2015 period when I was going to school. I came up with titles and premises that I really liked but because I just didn't have the momentum, they still sit there, in a notebook, in a drawer. I don't want to abandon that title or that story, but somehow, they feel distant from me. It's been really hard—call it impossible—to get back to them.

But if I can get the hang of doing a novel (or at least a first draft) in a month or two, that 'coasting to a full stop' won't happen.

Today, my goal is 4,000 words. That's a lot, I know, but I have the day all to myself. David is away on an errand to Savannah.

Writing this journal is getting me pumped up each morning to get to the computer and get the story told.

Day 4

I got close. Yesterday, I wrote 3,020 words.

Word count is part of the whole approach, but just as important, the ideas are flowing. I'm adding to the outline almost hour by hour.

The first idea that came in, on this novel, was the title. I got started on this *Media Mysteries* series in 2013 and drafted the first one, set in a TV station. I also had the idea that this series would use animal sayings for titles, the way Sue Grafton used the alphabet. *The Lion's Share of the Air Time* was the first one, published in 2015.

Next, I wanted to do one about movie production, and when I decided the setting would be Savannah, Georgia, where I was living at the time, I wanted to use birds, both in the title and as a key element in the plot. So, a bird in the hand became *A Bird in the Sand*.

For the third novel in the series, I decided on *Sleeping Dogs Lie*. The modification is to leave off the word 'Let', which is part of the actual saying.

I haven't worked out all the plot yet, but somehow the 'sleeping dogs' will be secrets. Lillian, the main character, wants to let them lie, or 'sleep', but her young friend, Chelan knows that they need to be 'awakened. For Lillian's health—perhaps even her survival.

Another angle on it is the double meaning of 'lie'. The secrets are a lie, somehow. Lillian's belief about the secrets from her past is a mistaken, harmful belief.

These ideas get filtered through the story, too, which is about literal, actual dogs.

Lillian was a sort of sidelined, occasionally catalyst character in the first two books. Well, in the second book, she was. In the first —
SPOILER ALERT

In the first book she was a mysterious woman, living in her car, poverty-stricken, untrusting of people. She receives a gift of money in a bequest and this enables her to move to Florida. She seems happy. But in this new book, as the plot is evolving, I think I'll have her be a lonely newspaper columnist, unwilling to befriend people.

So, the first idea was to do Book 3, about a newspaper and about Lillian. Next, it was to be a small town in Florida because that's what I know these days.

I saw an article about an upscale dog training facility that tries to teach non-natural behaviors. For example, some people want the trainer to teach their poodle to be a sheep-herding dog. I want to incorporate that in some way.

I also knew I wanted to make this a mystery with no explicit violence, no explicit sex, no foul language, and with an amateur sleuth searching in a small, closed community. The first book in my series had murders, the second had thefts, and I thought I'd work with 'what if ... the murderer targets a dog'.

This one idea sets up the flow of so many others. For a while, I was flailing around, trying to decide: Who gets killed? Do we (the readers) like him or her or not? Do we care? Why? How does Lillian get involved in investigating?

But once I had the initial idea, everything flowed. Lots of supplementary ideas. What's that first idea called? The 'launch' idea?

Day 5

Before I started, I spent some time analyzing where to do the work. I have a desk in a home office but it is the place where I make appointments, pay bills, make plans, etc. It seemed too practical and too connected to 'daily chores' for something as glamorous as a new novel.

I like to sit on the couch (and let's be honest, stretch out on the couch) and I do a lot of writing there. I will probably, when all is said, done, and written, spend a majority of the NaNoWriMo time, working there.

I decided to set up official shop on the dining room table. It has bookshelves on one wall, and it's very inspirational, to see all those books and the efforts of all of those other writers. I've done a lot of the pages there.

But I haven't been feeling one hundred percent this week, and so I've been gravitating back toward the couch. It's just a bit of a cold, with some headaches and a sore throat. I think I'm a bit rundown and tired out from the week before November, when we made a business trip to Indianapolis. Airports, hotel, travel food, and not enough sleep.

It's not been enough to stop me, but it has slowed me down. I had some thoughts, at the start of this month, that I might find a place away from home to work some of the time—a library, a café, even a park bench. That still might happen in the weeks to come but for this week, the couch is my choice of 'where?'

Day 6

I am definitely noticing that I've slowed down compared to Day 1. It's been easier for the distractions to take over, too.

I haven't been feeling terrific, but so far, I've been able to overlook that and keep turning out these words. It's not necessary to feel one hundred percent, but it certainly makes it easier to turn my full attention to the novel.

I'm also finding myself at the "let's start over" point. I've run up against this before: I start off on something, full of enthusiasm for it. Then, a little time passes, and I realize the story that's turning up on my pages isn't anywhere near as "pretty" as the one I saw in my mind.

I have some new ideas and they seem better than the one I'm working on now. Let's start over!

But I know that's just procrastination. Maybe some fear, too. Fear that my story won't be good enough and that I won't have the stamina or the smarts to finish it.

Day 7

Today, I left the writing in this journal to the end of the day, as an experiment. Some days, I've been feeling that I've poured out so much into the journal, in the first half hour of the day, that I don't have that itch to write and it's hard to get going on the novel.

It was easier to get to the writing today, after not doing the journal. But, on the other hand, this journal entry is going to be short! I'm drained.

I think I'll try alternating between the two schedules.

Today I wrote about 2,000 words. I'm at a total of 17,500. Almost to the end of Part One. I think this project will go much longer than the 50,000 words they state as the guideline for calling the novel "finished".

Day 8

Nearing the 20,000-word mark and I think that later today I will check out the social aspects of NaNoWriMo. So far, I've stayed very focused, even wary about letting myself be pulled 'off-task' by all of the entertaining, educational, or comforting alternatives there might be.

The NaNoWriMo site has various online meetings going on almost every day. They're called "Write ins" and are sponsored by various groups supportive of writers or wanting to get in front of writers: libraries, teachers, coaches, agents.

I haven't signed up for any of these yet. The one that interests me is the Hatha Yoga/Writing Prompts session. I'm curious about which one you do first—or maybe you do a little bit of this, then a little bit of that?

Writing can be hard, and I think a lot of us look for distractions or ways to procrastinate. If we're not actively looking, we might be receptive. I think that's probably why less than 11 percent of registrants will "win" and will finish the 50,000 words.

It's odd, because my mind runs about 18 or 19 hours of the 24, seven days a week. If I just write down the stream going through my brain, it's easy. Once I break the ice or get it melted or whatever, it's just a matter of 'taking dictation' and writing down everything that flows on by. That's what I'm doing now.

But as soon as I start to apply any sort of structure (plot, characters, theme), writing becomes much harder. The questions multiply: does this phrase sound natural? Who is speaking? What's the point of view? Past tense or present? Where does this scene fit in?

I'm sitting on my balcony in the Florida sunshine, trying to decide whether my sunscreen is doing its job. Again, my mind is welcoming any reason to turn aside and think about anything other than my novel.

Distraction is a beast.

Day 9

The weather is changing and it's getting colder. (Ha! In Florida, the idea of 'colder' is 61 degrees.)
Is it a sign that I'm losing interest in this novel, that my mind is turning to observations about the weather?

No, I hear from many writers that it's common to have phases of self-doubt during a substantial project like writing a novel.

Yesterday, I 'killed off' a character because I felt like the action was slowing down and something dramatic needed to happen. But today, I'm thinking I'll revive him because it really wasn't the right thing to do at that point in the story.

I woke up this morning with a thought: let the characters do things, watch them, and let them drive the action. I've read that, as a piece of advice, and it really does work. For example, this novel I'm working on is a murder mystery, set at a community newspaper office, and I created a group of four reporters and photographers. We've seen them at one meeting but I haven't done anything else with them, and I should. In a way, they're shouting at me that it's time to give them some center-stage moments.

So today, Bobby, Angela, Carrie, and Ben will go to work, talk to each other, show us life at a newspaper and we'll see what they come up with.

Day 10

Can I do 7,000 words today?

That's the number I've come to as a goal. I've never done as many as that in a day. My best so far is 5,020. I'm working through a very detailed outline (two versions are at the back of this book) and I'm refining it each day. It's been really helpful to do that. I go to bed each night, thinking about the scenes (which are numbered, crafted, and put into an overall structure) that I'm going to work on the next day.

Each scene is 1,000 to 2,000 words, and therefore I know how many I need to do in order to reach my word count goal for the day. When it's not NaNoWriMo, this process can stretch out over many days. I think the essential difference is that usually I wait for a good idea to come to me. Sometimes, I brainstorm dozens of ideas and scrap almost all of them.

But this month of November is more like my journalism days. No time for waiting for the 'best' idea to come to you. Just sit down and get it done.

Writing 3,000 words a day (or 1,667, which is the NaNoWriMo guideline to get to 50,000 words by the end of the month) is not that hard for one day. Even two, in a row.

But to do it, day after day! That's what I'm finding tougher. Nine straight days now. I've never produced two or three thousand words each day for nine days in a row. Never.

My train of thought is derailed.

Day 11

Today was a good day. I woke up at 2:30 a.m. with an idea for the B-plot and after about an hour of debating with myself, I got up to get down to the writing.

For years—decades, really—I've acted on the idea that if you can't sleep, it's a good thing. Don't lie there, tossing and turning. Get up and do something productive.

So, I put in eight hours of writing before lunch time, and got very close to 3,000 words today. At that pace I'll make it to 80,000 words by the 30th.

I had lots of interruptions later in the. A man came by, four hours earlier than expected, to work on the air conditioning. People out by the pool were having an afternoon party. I just put in earbuds, listened to music, and tuned them out.

I have a playlist on Spotify for this project. (I have one for every novel and travel book I've done.) This one has about twenty songs, all from 2015, which is the time setting for *Sleeping Dogs Lie*. Charlie Puth, Shawn Mendes, Meghan Trainor, Chris Stapleton, Adele, Ed Sheeran, Rihanna.

My B plot is turning into a problem child. At the moment, it has to do with celebrity. An F1 racecar driver has dogs that he brings to the trainer Lillian suspects is the killer. But I'm not sure the racing connection works, unless I loop in greyhound racing somehow. And that's so controversial. They've just finished (in 2018) banning it in 47 of the states and I don't want this mystery novel to take on a non-fiction, editorial slant.

I'll just have to let that one percolate for a while.

Day 12

I have a new idea. I'm going to have the B plot center on a super-model, instead. She's brought her dogs to Bouvier for training. She'll be an old friend of Chelan's, who comes to Alamos Island to visit her.

There's a parallel between show dogs and fashion shows that works better than Formula One racing.

It also solves the problem of where, how, and why an F1 driver would be in southwest Florida for any length of time.

I read a blog yesterday about NaNoWriMo and the participation in it. It was all about statistics, and how 370,000 novels were written that year—and it was 2012!

So, nine years ago, there were that many novelists. The number is probably much larger now, in the midst of a pandemic, when so many people have had their usual activities reduced or eliminated.

It's a bit daunting, this sense that so many people have done or are doing what I'm doing. This month of trying to do a complete first draft in 30 days is a massive, all-consuming focus for me. It fills the whole windshield.

But to NaNoWriMo, I'm just a tiny speck. One of 370,000 plus.

I'm not sure how I feel about that, or why it's significant, but it just feels like it is.

Another way of looking at it though, if I want to look at numbers, is that 350 million people (in the U.S.) have not written, or are not writing a novel in this one month, and I am.

I think the important thing is to avoid thinking about what other people are doing, and about what's going on elsewhere in the world. That's hard for me because of my former job as a journalist. I don't know whether it was the journalism training that partly formed me or that I gravitated to journalism because I was/am inclined to watch and be influenced by other people.

Whichever, I have to work at not noticing how many others might be doing something and at not being intimidated by that. I need to just focus on my own goal, my project, my pleasure in writing.

I had a thought yesterday about writing, and why some days are difficult. Think of acting or singing. People don't say "I'm trying to act" or "I'm trying to sing". They just do it. Some people do those things well, some badly, but you just act or sing.

So, why do I think "I'm trying to write"? Probably because the rest of that sentence is "I'm trying to write amazingly well" or "I'm trying to write the best novel ever".

Another (and perhaps, better) way to go at it is to look at each of my writing sessions as a performance. Just as if I went on stage, there is a moment when the curtain rises, the lights go on, and I open my mouth to speak or sing.

Maybe that's a way to put the 'trying to write' roadblock behind me. I'll try that today.

Day 13

And 17 to go! Why isn't it possible to form an intention, set a goal ("I will write a novel"), put in a few days' work, and then wake up to find it done??!

Instead, after those few days, you put it aside, then pick it up again, then put it down, etc. etc.

Then, one day you wake up and realize that it's been seven or eight years since you started! This NaNoWriMo business shows you how to avoid that, and gives you the experience, rather than just the theory.

In the future, I think I will declare my own National Novel Writing Month, as a way of getting things done. Why couldn't March be Novel Writing Month, just for me? Or June or October?

David calls this MyNoWriMo.

Tomorrow, I tackle the midpoint sequence of *Sleeping Dogs Lie*. Three scenes take place at a dog show. Mayhem ensues.

Day 14

I've been thinking about printing out the pages of the manuscript at the end of each day. I've been doing this since Day 1, and the effect on the process has been really positive.

I hadn't expected that. In another way, it might be very rewarding (internally) to store up the pages and print them out in a whoosh at the end. Three hundred finished pages. Wow!

That's the way I usually do it and this is the first time I've done it, day by day. I like it. Each evening, ten to fourteen pages have been printed and added to a growing pile. I can see the physical evidence of all the work, and it motivates me to do more.

There have been a few times when I've made significant revisions to a section (too much to change by hand) and I've gone back to the doc, done the rewrite, then printed out that page and substituted it for the previous one.

And this has also been a good discipline for making sure I don't get stuck on revisions, going back over and over the same pages and chapters, or tweaking one or two sentences.

Or name changes! That's another one where I can rethink and stew over the best name for a character. Sometimes, that improves things and it can take time to land on the absolutely perfect name. But it's also a great time-waster, playing with names.

And if you change it, but don't catch it on every reference in the doc, suddenly, after chasing Joe all through the book, the reader can't figure out why the protagonist is confronting Tom.

Thank goodness for Find and Replace.

It must have been so difficult, in the old days, when people worked on typewriters and they had to read and reread to find those errors, then retype the pages to use the new name.

These days, we can easily make the changes, and they're often for the better. Better pacing, better thematic development, better character arcs. But little changes, like the spelling of a name, are often unnecessary. Not always, and yes, finding the perfect name for a character or a place is always a goal. But sometimes, the change is not an improvement.

And what about the times I've changed it, then changed it back, then changed it back again?!

Pure procrastination.

The momentum of this month has helped me move past that. Printing the pages every night helps me stick with choices that have been made and don't need to be re-made.

Last night, I got to page 109. I have two more days to go to the halfway point of the month, and I'd like to get that number up to 130, at least. Up to 150 pages, ideally.

Time to get busy.

Day 15

Today, I am still mired in the midpoint sequence. I've learned a lot about structure in the past year from Savannah Gilbo and K.M. Weiland. Watching movies, I see the beats play out. The midpoint is often the point where I decide whether I think it's a good movie or not. It's the same as with a book, when you decide at some point whether you care about the characters or how it ends.

So far, I am still avoiding the social aspects of NaNoWriMo. I'm already thinking I might like to do this again next year, but make time for the online webinars, chat sessions, even the yoga classes. My first priority was to achieve the word count goal and to finish *Sleeping Dogs Lie,* not just have it dribble off at 50,000 or 52,000 words, partway through Act 3, unfinished.

But once I know I can do it, it might be fun to meet some new people and some other writers this way.

Day 16

Today, I discovered a badge I won't be getting. Arrgh! For OCD types like me, part of the 'success' of the NaNoWriMo method has been about showing up every day and claiming the online badges that they award for 5,000, 10,000, and 25,000 words, etc. You also get a badge for updating your results every day, and for seven days in, 14 days, and 21 days.

But today I found out there is a badge for doing the minimum average words need to win, (50,000 words / 30 days = 1,667), each day and every day.

Some days, I do 3,000 or 3,500, but I've had a couple of days when I've done 1,000 or 1,500. Still pretty good, I think, but because it's not up to the 1,667, no badge.

Arrgh!

Day 17

A change in the routine. David is to give a presentation in Austin, Texas tomorrow afternoon, so we're traveling this morning.

Six a.m. flight out of Fort Myers, Florida. Arrival in Austin at 12:30 (11:30 local time). Then, an hour's drive to a resort where the meeting is. Seven hours of travel time (plus forty-five minutes to the airport).

I don't know yet whether I'll get any new writing done today but I'm going to try. I think I'll try first on the plane, because you really are a captive there. I know, there is plenty of distraction with the seatback entertainment system and tons of movies to watch (not to mention, the books I have on my phone).

And that might be what I do. But I'm going to give writing a shot.

Another element is the proximity to other people. Will I be able to get into the zone with someone right beside my elbow and twelve inches away from my laptop screen?

If it's David, though, that will be okay. More than okay.

Day 18

I am now doing Version 4 of my outline.

Part of the NaNoWriMo deal is you're allowed to prepare an outline, character sketches, setting descriptions, and general planning notes beforehand.

I thought I'd done that. But I've found, over the past three weeks, things are changing as I go along.

They're not *major* things, though. The premise is the same, and so are the main characters and the plot. But within each chapter and scene, things are changing, and so is the order of the scenes.

Day 19

Our three-day business trip to Austin is ending today.

It's been a challenge to keep the writing going. Difficult, but not impossible. I've done many fewer words than usual, and had many more self-doubts.

But overall, there's been progress.

Day 20

Today, I wrote my second-highest number of words. 3.808.

I am getting close to the end of Act 2 (which is actually Part 3). The saddest, toughest part of the story. From here, Lillian starts to work harder, overcome more challenges, and drive toward the finish line.

I took a break to look at my social media and email. A mistake. Someone at the Florida Writers Association had blogged about NaNoWriMo being a dumb idea—putting too much "pressure" on yourself, while diving into a project that isn't long enough (50,000 words) for a "real" novel anyway, and besides, who knows if they will be "good" words.

It made me furious. I almost wrote a comment, then realized that would mean the cynic won. I didn't need the distraction and I didn't want to let someone else get inside my head.

It also made me want to write my own blog about NaNoWriMo. This would be a piece by someone who actually did it, and won it, not by someone who had an opinion but no experience (remember the teacher who knows a hundred ways to make love, but no women or men). I could write about the benefits, the costs, the highs, and the lows.

I was happy with myself that I didn't let that blog pull me off course. The three days on the business trip didn't throw me off, either. I think I've learned to direct myself better and maintain concentration.

I'm up to 40,000 finished words now. I think the draft will be about 70,000 when I get to The End. I'm on target to be done November 30th.

Yay!

Day 21

When I started the month, I decided not to read any other books or watch any movies, to avoid being influenced by others' tone or intimidated (or depressed) by their achievements.

But as the weeks have gone by, I've amended that. I *am* watching some movies and TV series. Staying very conscious about not 'borrowing' any themes or details. It's not been that hard to do, actually, because my own story is so clear and firm.

It was a wonderful break and a rest, I discovered, to leave the dog mystery in south Florida behind for a few hours for a screen 'trip' to Christmas time in England. Last night, I watched *Love, Actually*. Five weeks to Christmas!

It also makes me feel collegial and surrounded by other writers and creatives. I'm a writer, too! And one who is right in the midst of thirty days in a row, writing 2,000 to 4,000 words each day!

Day 22

Today, I reached 50,000 words! It felt very good—and yet, this also feels like the longest month ever. I want to be at the real finish line, when I type The End regardless of what the word count is. Getting from the beginning point to that finish line is LONG.

I understand why so many people don't finish!

When I put in the updated word count on the NaNoWriMo website, and it was over 50,000, digital confetti blew across the screen, with the word Congratulations!

Then I ordered a Winner T-shirt. I might be sixty-seven, but I'm still a kid.

Day 23

I made very little progress today. It wasn't that the number of words was that small (it was more than 2,000) but it took *hours* to get there.

And I had a feeling throughout the day that the quality was poor: that I was just filling pages with lines of text, working through the next steps of my outline without any spirit or excitement about it.

I shut down midafternoon and I just couldn't get back to it later.

Day 24

Still feel in a rut today. Only a few hundred words so far. I've been distracted, distractible, not able to concentrate. Is this all because of hitting that 50,000-word mark? Has it screwed me up, psychologically?

1:30 p.m. I think I'm finally back on track. It took 48 hours.

Day 25

Thanksgiving Day in the U.S. Quite a distraction from novel-writing. But November **is** the month for NaNoWriMo. Either I can stay hyper-focused on the novel and curb my interest in Thanksgiving, Veterans Day, and a lot of Christmas and Hannukah preparation, or let my attention wander to those and not finish the novel.

NaNoWriMo is international, so perhaps the timing of the main month works for people in countries other than the U.S.

But, maybe, no matter what month they chose, there would be interruptions and distractions.

Maybe I should just declare my own MyNoWriMo next year. January? March? June? August?

If I plan for that, and commit to that, does that mean I can pull the plug on this tub full of writing in November 2021?

No.

Day 26

I realize that I write every day but I don't always write fast. So, the change I need to make is to write fast and just let the draft come out as messy as it wants to. No agonizing over each sentence or word. No changing a character's name a dozen times.

Get the target number of words or the scene rolling out the way I want it to. After it's all out there, on the page, I'll go back and revise. Perfectionism is the enemy.

Day 27

The T-shirt came today! NaNoWriMo Winner 2021. It means 50,000 words. But I won't feel like "I Did It!" until I've done each of the thirty days **and** fully finished the novel.

Day 28

The three last days! I'm so in the groove now. Yesterday and Friday, I was working on the showdown scene, when Lillian gathers together all the suspects (and the reader) to reveal the killer. I feel more momentum in the story-telling!

Still some plot holes though, and today will be about fixing them.

Then, I'm going back to the "high tower scene". My MC isn't in quite enough danger. I haven't quite figured out whether that will be literal, physical danger, psychological, spiritual, or metaphysical.

Then, I'll write the "a-ha moment" scene when MC figures it all out.

That leads into the showdown scene, which is already written.

Then, I'll get to print out the pages. One of the motivators (and pleasures) has been printing out the daily five, ten or fourteen pages each evening. But this week, when I got into the 'jigsaw' approach, I realized I had to stop printing out pages because the pagination would be all off, if I printed the last thirty before the preceding thirty-something.

But I've missed the 'reward' of doing that each day and I'm looking forward to getting back to it, once the high tower surprise scene is done.

Day 29

Such a temptation to coast to the finish line! Interesting. There's also a bit of a sense of fatigue with my story. I've thought it through so many times that I think I'm bored with it.

With the entire genre, actually.

I'm thinking, (while I *should* be thinking about dialogue, setting, and transitions) —"I've done mystery, what else could I do? Ooh, how about paranormal romance? Werewolves, vampires, ghosts? That would get the writer adrenaline going!"

I want to change the genre, and I want to change this story, too. I know the ending now, and how to get there. Writing it, sentence by sentence, is the hard part. Telling is much easier. Why don't I just do that? Or use point form to get to The End?

Because I shouldn't. And I won't. Two more days and I will, for real, have every word and page of the first draft done, as good as it can be, at this point.

Then, I will rest it for three weeks or so, then start to work through the thirty-seven major revision points I have listed. So far.

Day 30

The last one!
I had a major boost that's helped me get through this last day and finish these scenes. I had an offer to traditionally publish a novel I submitted a few months back!

I am so thrilled!

But I'll be careful not to let this derail me from my last day on NaNoWriMo or from finishing the first draft of *Sleeping Dogs Lie* today. I'll look at the offer and the contract tomorrow.

For today, I will finish these last two scenes. They are important! And difficult. I have to get the clues and the revelations just right.

But I'm not going to let them intimidate me or bring me to a stop. If I don't get them exactly right, I can always go back later and fix them up.

I think it's important in NaNoWriMo to remind myself over and over againthat this is a first draft and it doesn't have to be perfect.

But it isn't *just* a first draft. If it weren't for first drafts, I wouldn't have anything real to show for all this time spent thinking about a novel or writing in general. Libraries would be empty, bookstores would be nothing but pretty shelves, and readers would be in shock.

This NaNoWriMo experience, with the challenge of a daily word count and the calendar 'box' of thirty days, has changed my habit of polishing repeatedly (sometimes, endlessly) and re-starting frequently.

About six o'clock today, I typed those words The End.

Feels so good.

Epilogue

December 2021

Revisions to *Sleeping Dogs Lie* were a major focus for this month (in addition to celebrating holidays, of course).

As I went through writing the story last month, I left gaps when I had no inspiration—for a character description, for example, or a name or a bit of dialogue.

This jigsaw puzzle approach left me with a lot of 'fill in the missing pieces' to do.

Also, I was working to a tight deadline. I had set up an ebook preorder on Amazon for January 7. That meant I had about five weeks to do the revisions, design the interior layout, plan a cover, and upload everything.

So, it was a busy December.

For the cover, we used a photo I took at sunset at Mackle Park on Marco Island, one of the settings for the novel. It is a beautiful line of palm trees silhouetted against the last of the daylight, at the edge of a small lake. (Beautiful, but sinister somehow).

The next one of the Media Mystery series that I'll write will be *Red Herrings Radio*. It will actually be Book 6, the last one of this series. It tells a story from Lillian's point of view, beginning with her receiving an old friend's diary in 2019, then remembering events from 1964 when that friend was killed in Toronto.

After that, I plan to get into the first draft of Book 4 of the series, tentatively titled *Kangaroo Court*. It's a story told from Chelan's point of view, the same as in Book 1, *The Lion's Share of the Air Time*.

I enjoy all of this thinking about new books I want to write, but I realize it was also a way of distracting myself from the work involved in revising this first draft.

I did finish the revisions in time for January 7, and *Sleeping Dogs Lie* is now out there, making its way through the world.

Epilogue again

August 2022

Sleeping Dogs Lie has been named to the short list of the Florida Writers Association Royal Palm Literary Awards in the published Mystery category. The winner will be named October 29—after this book is published.

If you're curious about how it turned out, follow the WindWord Group on Instagram @windwordpandm, on Twitter @windwordpublish, or sign up for my newsletter at https://www.gailhulnick.com.

MY NANOWRIMO JOURNAL April 2022

Day 1

This time, I'm doing it in April when the beautiful weather outside, the new life, and the springtime vibe beckon in a way that they don't in November.

But it's underway! I have a good outline (maybe a little short on details) and lots of enthusiasm for this. I've been thinking about this series for many years. The first book, *The Lion's Share of the Air Time*, took me two years of actual writing and then four months of self-publishing. Book 2, *A Bird in the Sand,* was done from 2014 to publication in 2018 (and won a Royal Palm Literary Award in the Mystery category). Book 3, *Sleeping Dogs Lie,* was written in one month. Book 6, *Red Herrings Radio,* was written in a month and a half, with revisions planned for late next fall, taking time for comments from beta-readers on this one.

Book 5 is just a great black hole out there somewhere in the universe.

But Book 4, *Kangaroo Court,* got its start today! Three thousand thirty words done. I worked at the Marco Island Public Library; it was a good place to settle in and start some storytelling.

I'm pleased with Chapter 1. It's a good plunge into the social media world that is the focus of this one. The point of view is from the youngest of the three 'media ladies'. Chelan is thirty-two now, with a two-year-old child and a three-month-old baby.

This time, on Camp NaNoWriMo, I'm going to do some of the community interaction stuff. There was a one-hour 'forum' from four to five pm today with long list of participants. Very few commented. The idea was to use a writing prompt, to get yourself rolling (put the word 'pranks' somewhere in your story, and have one character lie to another).

A great way to break through any block you have about what to write. Prompts always are.

Maybe there were few comments because people were busy writing, not chatting.

Day 2

Day 2 is always more difficult. For anything—training for a run, starting a new course, writing at novel at NaNoWriMo. The excitement and pent-up energy for Day 1 is gone and the reality of the commitment is sinking in. *Thirty days like this?!*

Twenty-nine, actually. It's just a matter of adjusting the thinking. Tighten the focus, go day by day, and don't take the bird's-eye view.

And count the Done days. One Done and in the bag.

Today was harder than yesterday at the library, but even working at home, I got the minimum 1,667 words and blew past that to 2,000.

For me, 1,667 isn't enough. I won't finish this novel at that pace. The guideline of 50,000 words for a novel is too short and I need at least 2,500 a day to get me to 75,000 words for this story.

After today's writing was done, I attended the virtual Pitchapalooza put on by The Book Doctors, a husband-and-wife team of book coaches who guide writers through the processes of developmental editing, crafting queries and proposals, pitching agents and publishers, and marketing the book.

For six weeks before NaNoWriMo, they received pitches from previous NaNoWriMo winners. They chose 20 of them and today will do a webcast with a critique of each and advice to the writers on how to make their pitch even better as they get ready to put it in front of a literary agent or an acquisitions editor at a traditional publishing house.

It was energizing and motivating to hear all of those pitches. So many good ideas and so many people who love to write! One came from a fifth-grader who was part of an entire class whose teacher had them in NaNoWriMo last fall.

It was very international, too, with participants from the UK, from Australia, and from Denmark.

What happens next? The twenty pitches are posted on the website and the people currently in Camp NaNoWriMo can vote for their favorites.

I think I'll try to get in on this for next fall. Finish *Kangaroo Court*, revise, and write the pitch over the summer? It's a possibility, although at the moment I'm still ambivalent about the choice between pursuing a trad pub deal and continuing to do the publishing job in addition to the author job.

I decided against taking the contract offered earlier this year by a publisher who wanted to sign me. It just required me to give too much away, take too much risk, and invest too much in doing my own marketing. I do get it, that publishers are under a lot of financial pressure. Everyone with a role to play in the process—bookstore, distributor, printer, publisher, and author (not to mention the agent, the editor, the cover designer, the interior designer, the publicist, the freelance sales rep, the librarian, the literary associations)—is under financial pressure, with a pie that is shrinking, while more slices are cut into it every year.

Some days, it seems to make the most sense to me to do as much as I can on my own, and therefore keep more than the two to three percent that a traditionally published author is often offered these days (and increasingly, with no advance offered, even by reputable, non-vanity publishers). Other days, I yearn for the freedom to spend my hours creating novels and improving my craft, and I'm willing to give up income and control over the cover, the title, and the marketing strategy, in order to focus on being the writer.

If I step forward with *Kangaroo Court* for next November's Pitchapalooza, I know I should have this uncertainty sorted out. "Umm, I might like to sell you my book or get on board with you as a partner, bu..u..t I think I might like to indie-publish instead." Wouldn't go over well.

The Book Doctors also mentioned that they're developing a reality show about writers competing for a publishing contract. After watching *Survivor, American Idol, The Voice,* and the *Amazing Race* for all of these years, now that I think about it, maybe it's high time there was a competition show about authors. There certainly are millions of them who would like the attention and the monetary rewards, just as there are singers, performers, and others who are just trying to live what they see as their 'best life'.

But, would it work for writers? The show producers alluded to this, when they were describing the hoops they jumped through to get TV producers interested. What would we be watching, a dozen writers hunched over computers or strolling through a park, gazing up into the clouds? The plan, apparently, is to have the writers, selected from a pool of applicants (large, no doubt), live together for a month in a house with the task of completing a short novel in that month. They're probably going to try to bake in as much time for personal conflict and emotional journeys as they can. I'd watch that—although I certainly would never want to be in it. Too many introvert urges going on over here. I think I read somewhere once that there's a higher percentage of introverts among writers than in the general population (and certainly, compared to stage performers and singers). Maybe my assumption that there would be a large pool of applicants is incorrect.

Day 3

Went a lot slower today.

I've got a good premise and that sent Chapters 1 and 2 on a good stride, lots of momentum. But now it gets harder. I need more story, more ideas, more developments, more characters.

Blech. What's on TV?

Day 4

Set up at the library to work again today. Apparently, it is the seniors' meeting place today. The parking lot is full and almost every table has people reading or playing games.

There are two Mahjong tables. They're fairly quiet and so are the group puzzle tables. It's only half an hour till lunch now. Maybe we'll get the place back to ourselves then. I wonder if it's just Monday or if it's like this every morning? The first time, on a Friday, we came in after twelve o'clock, so maybe we missed the rush? I know some writers like the collegiality of having other people around. I'm easily distracted, I guess. To be really productive, I need quiet—even silence.

Day 5

Someone asked me the other day "What does NaNoWriMo do for you that you can't accomplish on your own?"

Good question. I do love to write, I do it almost every day, why don't I just track my own word count?

I do track my word count, and after Camp NaNoWriMo is finished, I will continue to do that. But on a lot of days, I am distracted. I write two or three hundred words, then I feel I have to check my email, take a look at my schedule, or cross off one or two publishing tasks.

Then there are the steps even farther away from Writing My Novel: I might have a new book by an author I admire; there might be a screen adaptation of a book I've read; or my book might need at least a day's research into an important question.

If I spend some time doing those things, that's all still writing, isn't it? All part of the job, right?

So, I might get only three hundred words that day. It's been a good day, but the writing tally is small. At that pace, one draft of the novel will take 250 days. That's about eight months.

And that's only a first draft! There are still many more months needed for editing, revisions, copyediting, revisions, proofreading, revisions.

It's not that I'm impatient. But one thing I learned, while doing my first few books, was that I changed, sometimes in small ways and sometimes in ways not so small, during the years between putting down the first words and typing The End. I felt I wanted to go back and start all over again. I've heard from other authors that this is a very common feeling, and that the best thing to do is carry on. Do the next novel and don't spend any time stewing over how you would do that other one differently.

It seems to me that it's logical that if you write the novel in a few months, rather than years or decades, it will be a more accurate, vivid rendering of where your mind and heart are at the time of that writing.

The discipline of doing NaNoWriMo helps a lot.

Day 6

I am doing this journal entry at the beginning of the day, in order to kickstart things.

It was either that or two blueberry muffins.

This morning, I'm pondering whether it is better to set a word count target or a time count. I do better with a word count because I'm distracted by research and can fill three hours easily just roaming around the internet.

I'm thinking about first drafts and how I shouldn't expect perfect paragraphs to just pour out of me, first time, every time. Someone once said that it's like having a sandbox. You bring in those big bags of sand, then shovel them in. That's your first draft. **Next,** you add water and start to build things.

Day 7

The challenge of transitions.

I find it really difficult to stop one activity and move on to another. I remember when my kids were small, that was a common occurrence for them, too. Maybe it's my inner child that has trouble with this?

If I'm reading, it's tough to put the book aside and get down to writing. If I'm writing and I have to stop, for a meal or an appointment, I delay that transition, too.

Day 8

One week in! I've written every day, but missed the daily minimum target of 1,667 words on Wednesday, Day 6. Oh, well, so that's one badge I won't get. Last November I missed two—that one and the every day writing badge.

At first, on Wednesday when I got home from a dinner out, I thought of returning to my computer at 10 p.m. to try to get to the daily target. Instead, I decided to take the evening off and accept the badge missed.

Maybe I'll get them all next time. Gives me one more reason to sign up next November!

Day 9

Trying out a writing sprint today. This is not something that I have done much in the past. Keeping the flow of words going hasn't been a challenge.

But I'm a bit sluggish today. I'm going to do some 45-minute sprints. No distractions, no research, google or email. No kidding myself that because I have one millennial character in my story I need to stop to read the intriguing blog about 57 dating terms that millennials use.

In the past, my routine has been to sit down at this desk at 10 a.m. or so, and stay there until 4 or 5, with breaks for food and exercise. The pace is about the same, all day.

Today, I'll chop up the time into 45-minute blocks and write intensely during each one.

In my next life, maybe I'll be an expert in time management.

Day 10

A day with many distractions and interruptions. Plus, ten new ideas for novels and short stories.

I put them all in the "parking lot", a folder on my desktop where I put every idea that feels worthwhile but has the potential to pull me off the project I have underway.

Day 11

Now, I'm officially into the second third of the month. For time management purposes, I'll divide it into bite-sized pieces. Daily, I need at least 2,000 words, and on some days, I'll want 3,000.

If I think of each third of a month, I want 25,000 words in each 10-day block. This time, I'm at 20,400 at this point. That's behind where I was at this point in November.

I've also realized that there are two badges I won't get. I had one day this month when I did only 240 words.

But I'm still on track for updating and recording my results every day, even though on some of the days those results were unimpressive. The next badges I can grab will be for updating 14 days in a row and for reaching 25,000 words.

Day 12

My results this month aren't as strong as they were in November. I'm about four thousand words behind where I was November 12th.

I think that's because I paid a lot of attention to the outlines I was using and because I did a lot of preparation during October. I really knew my story, in my mind, inside and out, in November. This month, I've been pantsing it a lot more.

Some people do better with 'discovery writing', but I seem to need that structure.

Day 13

That bummed me out, to discover that I'm 4,000 words off my pace of last November. I will shake it off, but the psychological ups and downs of NaNoWriMo are an interesting thing.

It's very easy to get sidetracked and low-energy due to feelings of being inadequate for this task. Am I just wasting my time?

Day 14

Ideas on editing that I heard today (to use on a later draft):
- Print out the manuscript in a different, even unusual font. Every word will pop
- Print out a different title page, with a made-up (or famous) author's name. See whether it will change the mindset you bring to the reading
- Read it out loud. Use your software's read-aloud feature
- Let it sit for a week or more then read it through without stopping or making notes
- Then, read it through again, without stopping, but making notes on what you really liked about it
- Read it again, stopping only to make notes on things you intend to revise
- Make those substantive revisions, then do a copy edit and then a proofread.

Day 15

Craft thoughts today. I've been dwelling a lot on voice. It's important to make sure each character has their own voice. And that the overall book has a voice. I think of actors and how they create a character, adopting a voice, but still maintaining their own, overall persona.

Day 16

So, you get a badge for posting every day. I was in the habit of doing that as the last thing. A sort of summarizing, a pat on the back, time for a cup of tea.

But a couple of times last November and now once (so far) this month, I've let myself get distracted and have missed a day.

My solution is to update at lunch break. I suppose I could do it whenever I take a break or reach a 'take stock' point in the writing. Could be the end of a scene in the story. Could be after two hours, after four hours, or whatever. Could be after I reach each 1,000 words. Whatever. The point is that day's post would be under my belt and not at risk of being forgotten.

I can update again at the end of the day, if I want (and if I remember).

Day 17

My 'planner' side took over today and I spent a lot of time polishing and revising my outline. Up to now, I'd been pantsing quite a bit, just going with the flow, in the moment. Discovery writing can be a lot of fun, especially with mysteries.

But I'm finding that I have scenes that are exciting, but don't lead anywhere. It almost feels like they belong in a different book.

Today, I added a lot of new ideas for scenes this book needs, and strengthened the ones I'd already thought of. The midpoint scene, for example, will be three scenes, at a neighborhood street party.

I also decided where and when to introduce a couple of key new characters.

But I didn't let myself get bogged down in the planning. I want to win NaNoWriMo and get those 50,000 words (and maybe some or most of the other 80,000 that I think I'll need for this story).

So, I have to keep that tap turned on. Keep writing and keep the flow going, even when I don't feel like it.

Day 18

I am finding April an easier month to work in than November.

Or, am I? Both months have a major holiday/feast day in the U.S., where I am this year: Thanksgiving/Easter. The weather in November can be more conducive to staying in, although in years like this one, with a late spring, that might not be true.

I'm up to 36,000 words this morning. Each day, I start out reaching. Today, I'd like to get to 40,000. That would make this my most productive day.

Day 19

S ome days, I'm convinced all this word counting hampers the quality of the writing. I certainly have let it become something to think about, other than the depths of my story.

But I don't know if I'd be able to think about a story that continuously, day after day. If I weren't thinking about word counting, maybe I'd be planning grocery lists, instead.

Day 20

N o time for the journal.

Day 21

S ame.

Day 22

S ame.

Day 23

J ust noticed the way that some writers are turning nouns into verbs lately: "he architected a plan"; "curls haloed her head".

My online editor yesterday (on another project) was pushing me to reduce the quantity of passive voice sentences in my paragraphs. Here's a way to do that! Change the nouns into verbs.

Day 24

Should I drop the project if I get sick halfway through the month? No! Write something every day, even if it's only 100 words. You shouldn't think "Oh, I couldn't possible write 1,667 words or spend three or four hours today, so I'm out."

You should think "I can write 100 words. I can keep the daily habit going."

If I take one day off, then I'm more likely to take two, and before you know it, the whole NaNoWriMo is botched.

Now, I'll miss one badge, maybe two. The ones for making the daily goal and updating every day. But I can still get all the others.

More important, I won't give up on the whole thing.

Day 25

No time for the journal.

Day 26

Same

Day 27

Same.

Day 28

No time for the journal.

Day 29

Lost a few days in the daily note keeping for NaNoWriMo, but I'm still working on it.

Some of the days when I was feeling low, my word count was low, too But I tried to keep up the stretch.

Unfortunately, I missed one day. I did write that day—about a thousand words—but I forgot to update my NaNoWriMo page. Just an oversight. Too much to do.

So, there it is. But I don't mind too much. Gives me motivation to sign up again next November and try to do all thirty days.

It will be a stretch for me, in the next two days, to make it to 50,000 words. But I'm all recovered from the surgery and I think I can do it. Goal is 2500 words a day on each of the two days.

Structurally, I'm past the midpoint and the novel should flow more easily now.

Day 30

Finished 50,454 words!

Not as many as in November 2021, but I made it to the minimum word count for winning NaNoWriMo.

And did it in a month when I had a little surgery!

Just discovered you can set your own goal on the website. If you were writing a 200,000-word fantasy or sci-fi epic, you could set it up to target a minimum 6,667 words a day, or whatever.

Maybe I'll try this in November 2022. (Choosing my own word-count goals, not writing 200,000 words in a month.)

Although I am planning a trip to a conference in Las Vegas November 14 to 18. Will it be too much distraction? Or would it be good to have the two tracks running simultaneously?

Hmmm....

Epilogue

June 1, 2022

I finished another 20,000 (ish) words on *Kangaroo Court*. The first draft is done now, to be left alone until the first developmental edit. Long enough for me to forget individual sentences, perhaps even entire plot points or characters.

The idea is to come at it like a new reader. Go through it entirely, once, without judging or making notes. Just reading. Then a second read, allowing myself to make notes.

Then, revisions. And I do this as many times as feels right. Then, a copy edit and two proofreads.

I use a mixture of AI editing tools, like ProWriting Aid and Marlowe, and people, like beta-readers and editors. My first reader is always my husband, David Stone, and I deeply appreciate the time he puts in and the brilliance of his comments.

Last Thoughts

I started out on the road to creating this book because I wanted to make something that could help other writers. I remember how difficult it was for me to call myself a writer, even in my own mind. I could certainly never say it out loud.

It seemed like just a dream, a goal far out of reach.

That was nine years ago. I had done some writing up to then but I'd never had the courage to dive in. Like many people, I wanted to be a writer and to have written a novel, but I just didn't get started. It was as if I expected there to be some kind of magic that would give me the skill and transform me into a writer, without having to learn or do enough.

I've written just over a million words since then and the word 'writer' is one I use to describe myself now. I got to that point simply by 'doing the doing'. I learned that you have to make that first leap, and then keep on swimming. The more you do it, the more you can do it.

Writing is like playing an instrument, dancing, or doing a sport. You have to practice every day.

When I discovered NaNoWriMo, I had a new tool for practicing and for channeling my creative drive and pure enjoyment of writing into the sort of discipline and structure that could help me get the thing done.

I hope it will do the same for you.

NANOWRIMO STATS

Year	Participants	Finishers	Percentage
1999	21	6	22%
2000	140	29	17%
2001	5,000	700	12%
2002	13,500	2,100	13%
2003	25,500	3,500	12%
2004	42,000	6,000	13%
2005	59,000	9,769	14%
2006	79,813	12,948	2%
2007	101,510	15,333	13%
2008	119,301	21,683	15%
2009	167,150	32,178	16%

2010	200,500	37,500	16%
2011	256,618	36,843	13%
2012	341,375	38,438	10%
2013	310,095	42,221	12%
2014	325,142	58,917	15%
2015	351,489	40,423	10%
2016	384,126	34,000	8%
2017	402,142	48,257	11%
2018*	450,000*	53,000*	11%

Source: NaNoWriMo

National Novel Writing Month

- **1999**: 21 participants and 6 winners (29%)
- **2000**: 140 participants and 29 winners (21%)
- **2001**: 5000 participants and more than 700 winners (~14%)
- **2002**: 13,500 participants and around 2,100 winners (~16%)
- **2003**: 25,500 participants and about 3,500 winners (~14%)
- **2004**: 42,000 participants and just shy of 6,000 winners (~14%). Total words written: 428,164,975
- **2005**: 59,000 participants and 9,769 winners (17%). Total words written: 714,227,354

100 Ways to Win NaNoWriMo

- **2006**: 79,813 participants and 12,948 winners (16%). Total words written: 982,564,701
- **2007**: 101,510 participants and 15,333 winners (15%). Total words written: 1,187,931,929
- **2008**: 119,301 participants and 21,683 winners (18%). Total words written: 1,643,343,993
- **2009**: 167,150 participants and 32,178 winners (19%). Total words written: 2,427,190,537
- **2010**: 200,500 participants and 37,500 winners (19%). Total words written: 2,872,682,109
- **2011**: 256,618 participants and 36,843 winners (14%). Total words written: 3,074,068,446
- **2012**: 341,375 participants and 38,438 winners (11%). Total words written: 3,288,976,325
- **2013**: 310,095 participants and 42,221 winners (14%). Total words written: 3,520,123,164
- **2014**: 325,142 participants and 58,917 winners (18%)
- **2015**: 351,489 participants and 40,423 winners (12%)
- **2016**: 384,126 participants and over 34,000 winners
- **2017**: 402,142 participants
- **2018**: 295,396 participants and 35,410 winners (12%). Total words written: 2,921,032,466[1]
- **2019**: 280,098 participants[2]
- **2020**: 383,064 participants[3]

Source is wikiwrimo.org

Camp NaNoWriMo

- **2011**: 6,400 July Participants, 6,236 August Participants, 1,755 total winners
- **2012**: 15,307 June Particpants, 12,859 August Participants, 3,579 total winners
- **2013**: 44,919 campers
- **2014**: 55,774 campers
- **2015**: 57,402 campers and 10,682 winners
- **2016**: 60,951 campers
- **2017**: 65,962 campers
- **2018**: 70,023 campers
- **2019**: 70,632 campers
- **2020**: 71,832 campers

Source is wikiwrimo.org

RESOURCES

BOOKS

I have listed some of my favorite books on writing craft and the writer's life. If you've read these already, you know why I've included them here. If you haven't, you might want to add them to your TBR pile for this winter.

On Writing – Stephen King
Emotional Thesaurus --Becca Puglisi and Angela Ackerman
Bird by Bird – Anne Lamott
The Artist's Way – Julia Cameron
Save the Cat – Blake Snyder
Writing the Breakout Novel – Donald Maas
The Writer's Journey – Christopher Vogler

WEBSITES AND BLOGS

The internet is full of websites about writing and blogs you can search or subscribe to. Some offer paid services. Some are communities where writers trade information and expertise.
Here are seven that I've used and found worthwhile:

Writer's Digest
   https://www.writersdigest.com/
Medium
   https://medium.com
Wattpad
   https://www.wattpad.com/
Reedsy
   https://www.reedsy.com
Association of Writers and Writing Programs
   https://www.awpwriter.org/
Daily Writing Tips
   https://www.dailywritingtips.com/
Jane Friedman
   https://www.janefriedman.com/

PODCASTS

I listen to five to ten podcasts about writing craft or publishing each week. Listed below are the ones I recommend most frequently. They aren't the only ones, by any means, but if you don't have any writing podcasts in your library, these are a good beginning.

The Creative Penn Podcast for Writers with host Joanna Penn
https://www.thecreativepenn.com

Helping Writers Become Authors with host K.M. Weiland
https://www.helpingwritersbecomeauthors.com

Fiction Writing Made Easy with host Savannah Gilbo
https://www.savannahgilbo.com

Six-Figure Authors with hosts Lindsay Buroker, Jo Lallo, and Andrea Pearson
https://www.6figureauthors.com

OUTLINE VERSION 1

These are included to give you a look at the way that I work with outlines. The columns and rows sometimes change but the essential structure stays the same.

These outlines are full of spoilers, so please don't read them if you intend to read my novel *Sleeping Dogs Lie*.

Scene	What Happens	Point/Beat/Purpose
	Lillian finds a body.	Act 1. Beginning state. Life is about being retired and left alone. Reader questions: who are these people? why is she in such danger? Why does she run? what will happen next?
2.	Donovan comforts and challenges her. States the lesson.	Theme scene
3.	L. wants to find the killer.	Set up – living alone, retired. Needs to change
4.	Neighborhood - doggy Beach	Set up - home
5.	Newspaper clan - downtown	Set up - work
6.	Dog clan – just Carl. Vet.	Set up - Play

	Pet store	
7.	L. publishes a column about dog killer	
8.	L.'s house is torched	Inciting incident
9.	A urges her to move to condo cty	Maybe beats
10.	Newspaper office.	
11.	Naples garden	
12.	Dog park	
13.	L. decides to move to condo cty	
14.	L. decides to want to go after killer/arsonist	Bridge into Act2
15.	Chelan arrives for a holiday with baby	Intro B plot
16.	Pickle ball.	Trying to solve the crime Beats. Fun & Games. Heading Down
17.	Condo cty card games. Dog club	Tries and fails to solve the murder
18.	Vet. Her own doctor, med issues	Again. Back story on L. On dogs. on Villains.
19.	Condo clan	Again . What MC wants
20.	Dog friendly café	Again
21.	Nevada arrives for a visit	Pinch point 1
22.	Everglades	

23.	Condo town hall meeting	
24.	Newspaper office	
25.	Dog hiking trail	
26.	Restaurant	
27.	Chelan and L's Vancouver secret	
28.	Dog Training Event or Show	Midpoint1- C plot character – will help L. get her want
29.	False victory	Midpoint2 – Big event within midpoint sequence – avalanche! danger!
30.	L's life in danger	Midpoint3 - live out the 'promise of the premise'
31.	Dog park	Twist
32.	Chelan adopted by the condo clan	Bad guys close in
33.	L is still rejecting them	Answers questions from Scene 1
34.		Pinch point 2
35.	L has a new plan. Fails	Add some humor. Between characters.
36.		
37.	Carl is attacked, left for dead	All is lost
38.		Dark Night
39.		Villain 3 – C plot

40.		
41.	Dog training place – all act 3	
42.		Epiphany – Decision to act
43.		Act 3. Lillian learning the lesson
44.	L decides to trust – Who?	Solving the mystery
45.	Donovan helping with Lesson 1	
46.	Chelan helping with Lesson 2	
47.		
48.		
49.		
50.		Ending state (Opposite to beginning) with people and working
54.		

OUTLINE VERSION 12

Sc	Ch	What happens	Total Words	Page
1	1	Lillian finds a body. Act 1.Beginning state. Reader questions: who are these people? why is she in such danger? Why does she run? what will happen next?	1203	1
2	2	L. and Arlo call the cops	3003	
3		Annie challenges L's belief that life is about being retired and left alone. Theme scene		
4	3	Newspaper family. L. wants to find the killer. Set up - work		
5	Ch3	Neighborhood. Vet, pet food store, park. Dog fam. Set up - home	5164	
6	Ch3	At doggie beach, L meets Selena who hates dogs. character with cynophobia, abnormal fear of dogs. Red Herring. Set up - play		

7	Ch3	L writes column about dog killing	7169	
7.	Ch4	Bobby asks L to investigate. N puts out a reward. Maybe beats	12,069	
8	Ch4/5	L.'s house is torched. Inciting incident	15,000	56
9.	Ch5	Rx. A urges her to move to condo cty. Donovan visits. Maybe beats		
10.	Ch 6	Newspaper office. Bobby asks her to investigate again		62
11.		Dog park clues. Trainer. Gerald. Police tell L about golf club, footprint. Will L try to solve the murder?	18,000	
12.	Ch 7	Condo Tour with Arlo	20,000	72
13.	Chapt .8	L. at dog park, seeing pups. End of Act 1. What causes her to commit?		74
14.		L. decides to want to go after killer/arsonist, move to condo.		
15.		Turtle research. Chelan calls. Intro B plot, supermodel Iris Learns about Zhivago and IRF	23,000	
16.	Chapt 9	Gulf Coast Garden. Meets tour guide Marlon who talks about golf. Tries and fails to solve the murder		

17.		Dog walk. Add true clue here in revision. Carl digs up medication bottle at park. L thinking about golf club. Tries again.		
18.		Condo. Meets dog lovers. invited to IRF		
19.	Chap 10	Newspaper office. Sees Bobby, interviews Barbara. Back story on L.	25,000	84
20.		Dog friendly café. Going over what she knows. L tries and fails again		
21.	Chap 11	Nevada calls. L visits IRF – 1. Meets Chelan's model friend, Iris. Is Chelan there? Pinch point 1 – N kidnaps G's dog		
22.		Condo - - town hall meeting. L declines help from Alec.		10 9
23.	Chapt er 13	Newspaper office – Bobby has everglades lead – breeder of both dogs. Add Column 2 - about Mr Hyde		
24.	Chapt 14	Lunch with Chelan., L invites C to Everglades for a drive, L is going to find breeder. Backstory		
25.	14/15	Everglades 1 –watch tour guide, see golf clubs in trunk. Leave card for breeder. say goodbye to Chelan	32,000	13 4

26.	Chap 16	Dog show – meet rival Ellison; birder Selena; Arlo; N; G; Zhivago; Marlon. Iris. Ellison and Gerald are rivals but 'friendly'. E is G's doctor. Connect Marlon and Zhivago. Midpoint 1		15 0
27.		False victory – L finds kidnapped Hyde. Blames Ellison. Midpoint 2		
28.		L's life in danger – chased by dogs. Midpoint 3 – live out the promise of the premise		
29.		Newspaper fam; phone call with Nevada, going over suspect list. Rx to midpoint		
30.		L's pilgrimage to Everglades. Breeder says Ellison knew or did what? L finds out useful in		
31.		L interviews Ellison. Bad guys closing in		
32.		Dog park, L sees Selena, she wants to help L, points L to Zhivago she is on meds for dog anxiety. Selena twist		
33.		IRF 2 – L interviews Zhivago. He denies. Bad guys		
34.		Bad guys closing in. L. backstory. Doggie day at Garden – 2 , L sees Iris there, they talk. Iris followed her there. Suspect Iris too.		

35.		L interviews Riccardo, last one to see Turtle alive. He points to Arlo, who also golfs. Riccardo rushes away to answer G's call. Pinch point 2		
36.		Real estate office. L has a new plan/prime suspect. Interviews Arlo. Fails. L is still rejecting condo family. Donovan calls – beat 2. L doesn't tell him about Iris.		
39		Tour office. interviews Marlon (golf club – motive?). L fails again –Marlon has no motive, but doesn't have an alibi		
40		Doggie beach – Iris is leaving. L says she knew all along, why didn't she reveal? answer comes in book 6, what L felt she owed Marv. Carl with L. B plot #3		
41.		L interviews Barbara and Gerald, who plants false clue about Ellison, says they are not enemies, he's my doctor, I'm on anti-anxiety meds. E sold a car a week ago – yes, it was a Bentley. B's reward? Carl with Lillian. Raise the stakes		
42.		L. talks with Nevada, is warned. Carl is attacked, left for dead. At dog park. All is lost	180	

43		Vigil at the vet's; police warn her to go under the radar. Donovan arrives. Dark night of soul. Epiphany. Decision to act.		
44.		Condo fam – L asks their opinions. Gather the team, gather tools. Act 3.		
		Column 4. L tries to think like a dog.		
45.		L goes to IRF with Annie, Alec & Kyra		
46.		Condo/dog fam disabled, L alone. L in danger L made homeless (mirror the fire) – followed, no guard dog, no team		
47.		L. gets dogs to help. But who is chasing her? She confronts Z. He seems to back off. Solving the mystery, seems like L has won, then big change		
48.		High tower surprise. L. in delirium, underwater? falls off cliff? Chelan will be helping with Lesson 2 don't be alone; D with lesson 1 – don't think old. L trusts… both fams		
49.		Rx to HTS. L in hospital – defeated. Nothing left. But she's learned. fams come to help. Calls from Nevada, Chelan, police. Vet brings in Carl. L makes a new plan.		

50.		Climax. Showdown scene – L goes to IRF, (or to Band G's house? confronts 6 suspects, identifies killer/henchman	220	
51		Cops take Gerald and Riccardo away		
52		L back at condo with friends		
53		L has time on the phone with N and C		
54		L and Carl		
55		L having a party at her house. Ending state opposite to beginning	250	

SEVEN STEPS CHECKLIST

I have one more tool for you to use. You could run through this on the eve of November 1st. You could even run through it at the beginning of each writing session.

I have my
1. Story idea firmly in mind: premise, main character, antagonist, theme
2. Writing place planned
3. Schedule organized
4. Distractions anticipated and blocked
5. Daily word count goal established and day's result recorded
6. Family, friends, and partners onboard
7. Self-care plans made and milestone celebrations planned

That's it! You're good to go. No one else can do this.

Write **your** novel.

ABOUT GAIL

Following twenty years as a broadcaster and interview host on public radio, Gail Hulnick is now the award-winning author of eight novels, five travel books, two self-help books, and a collection of short stories. She is also the host of a weekly podcast exploring the inner workings of creativity. She lives, works, and travels from southwest Florida.

ABOUT WINDWORD GROUP PUBLISHING & MEDIA

The WindWord Group is a micro-publisher that releases fiction and nonfiction books, and podcasts.

If you'd like to know more about our mystery and women's fiction titles, our presentation and writing series *You're On!,* our business marketing books, our self-help and personal development series, or our podcast *The Brainwave*, please visit https://www.windwordgroup.com/

We send out a free, monthly newsletter under Gail's name, offering news about upcoming publications, special pricing, giveaways of books and other treats, and feature articles on writing craft. If you'd like to be a subscriber, please fill out the form that pops up when you visit the website.

Gail is available, via video call, for school, bookstore, and library appearances, writing projects, and podcast consulting. In-person meetings or book signings can also be arranged. Please contact admin@windwordgroup.com